When the Hurting Is Too Much

When the Hurting Is Too Much

A Guide to Contemplative Prayer to Help You Walk with Grief

ANTONIO MÉJICO

Foreword by Angie Lizeth Cruz

RESOURCE *Publications* • Eugene, Oregon

WHEN THE HURTING IS TOO MUCH
A Guide to Contemplative Prayer to Help You Walk with Grief

Resource Publications
An Imprint of Wipf and Stock Publishers
199 W. 8th Ave., Suite 3
Eugene, OR 97401

www.wipfandstock.com

PAPERBACK ISBN: 979-8-3852-7838-1
HARDCOVER ISBN: 979-8-3852-7839-8
EBOOK ISBN: 979-8-3852-7840-4

VERSION NUMBER 04/28/26

DEDICATION

Mark, it has been over a decade since you left, and to this day, I can still hear your voice and feel your hug as if it were yesterday. I still see you occasionally in my dreams, and when I do, we laugh and joke and cook chicken on an open fire. The way you left hurt me one way. The way I miss you hurts me another. Through it all, I am grateful to have known you and considered you my brother. This book is for you, and others like you who struggle with the will to continue, as well as those who are left grieving in the wake of a sudden and painful loss. I have been told that grief is love persevering. I hope my grief helps you know how much you were loved when you were with us. I miss you, brother.

Contents

Acknowledgments

Mrs. and Mr. H.,

Thank you for accepting me as your fourth son. I know you have lost much in your lives, but you should also know that you have equipped me to give much to others. Thank you for your love, support, and guidance throughout the years. Thank you for shaping my sense of self-worth and my heart for justice. You are loved deeply, and I am honestly a better person because of the wisdom and love you have poured into me over the decades. I love you both.

Foreword

Grief stays with us. Over time, it becomes part of how we love, remember, and walk with God.

Those who live long enough with loss come to understand that grief does not move in straight lines, nor does it resolve itself according to a timetable. It returns in different seasons, through new milestones, and in moments we do not anticipate. Over time, grief becomes something we learn to live alongside, not as a problem to be solved, but as a presence that forms who we are, how we love, and how we come to recognize God's nearness to us.

I know this not only as a therapist, child welfare social worker, and grief scholar, but as someone whose life has been shaped by early and profound loss. Dr. Antonio Méjico offered me the honor of writing the foreword for this book, unbeknownst to him, on the twenty-sixth anniversary of my father's death. I lost my dad suddenly in a car accident. His death remains the most raw pain I have ever known. Every loss that followed in my life, including divorce, trauma, and rupture, echoed the grief that first shaped my heart as a child.

Grief does not disappear as we grow older.

It grows alongside us.

Just days before writing these words, I was gathering my three-year-old and ten-year-old for a drive to La Puente, my hometown, to pick up my mother for the holidays and to visit my father's grave. Each Christmas, we place decorations there, an act of remembrance I continue so my children can know their grandfather, even in his absence. It is one small way I carry meaning forward and allow love to have somewhere to go.

I gathered the mini Christmas trees, the small village houses, and the delicate handmade nativity set and drove the familiar forty-mile stretch to my father's resting place. As we made our way toward the grave site, my son asked, "Mama, how do you always know exactly which tree his grave is by?"

"I've been coming here since I was eleven, my love," I told him gently. "It's instinct now."

My confidence felt earned. After years of returning to these hills, I believed I knew how to do this, how to move through grief without being undone by it. I was there to place the decorations, to include my children, to honor my father. For a moment, I thought I had learned how to hold grief without it holding me.

We climbed the gentle slope and laid the decorations on the ground. As we began to clean the grave, red ants swarmed across my father's picture and name. My son tried to pour water to chase them away, but more appeared, preventing us from continuing our ritual. I called the cemetery office and asked for assistance. The response was brief: "It's dirt. There are going to be ants."

The surrounding graves were undisturbed, yet ants streamed from the soil onto my father's grave marker. I felt unsettled, then a familiar ache in my chest, a hollow between my heart and my breath. It was grief, stirred again. Not failure. Not regression. Simply grief, reminding me that it still lived here, too.

I felt a steady need to protect the small piece of stone bearing my father's name and face. I said, "I didn't choose to visit my dad every Christmas at a cemetery. If this is where I include him in my holidays, I do not want ants crawling over his grave as I try to lay a nativity scene."

As the attendant prepared to submit a work order, she asked, "What is your father's name?"

I paused.

I could not remember the last time anyone had asked for his name, nor a moment when I had spoken it aloud in defense of his dignity. For a brief instant, it felt as though his memory and his place in my life had become abstract after a lifetime of grieving. I felt both ache and pride as I answered, "Ricardo Cruz."

My children stood quietly beside me, holding the small Christmas decorations and watching their mother grieve, still, decades later. In that moment, I was reminded of an enduring truth. We placed the decorations carefully beside the grave marker, and my children arranged them with an innocence that felt holy. I did not want this moment to stain our ritual. My father was still included in the eve of our holidays, and there was a quiet joy in knowing that love, remembrance, and meaning were able to take shape alongside grief.

Grief may linger, but God endures.

It is in this space, where grief remains, where love still longs, and where God abides, that *When the Hurting Is Too Much* offers its deepest gift. This book does not promise an end to grief. Instead, it invites readers into a way of being with grief that makes room for meaning, presence, and a deeper, steadier kind of joy.

Dr. Antonio Méjico does not write to offer answers or spiritual platitudes. He writes to offer presence. In a culture that rushes people through grief or asks them to be strong, faithful, or "get over it," this book creates space. Space to breathe. Space to grieve honestly. Space to encounter God not as an explanation for suffering, but as a companion within it.

Grief can alter the way we draw near to God in prayer. We may struggle to find words, and silence can feel overwhelming. Dr. Méjico understands this terrain. He invites readers into contemplative prayer not as something to master or perform, but as a place to rest. A place where showing up tired, unsure, and aching is enough. In stillness, in listening, and in simply remaining present before God, something begins to mend, not because grief disappears, but because we are no longer alone within it.

What makes this book especially powerful is its respect for the long arc of grief. Dr. Méjico does not treat grief as a chapter to be closed, but as a lifelong relationship that evolves across seasons. This book gives readers permission to grieve again without shame and to discover that meaning and spiritual joy can coexist with sorrow.

The joy spoken of here is not happiness or relief. It is the quiet, anchoring joy that comes from knowing God remains near. It is a joy rooted in trust, formed through prayer, and sustained by presence. It is the joy that allows us to keep loving, keep remembering, and keep walking forward, even when our hearts still ache.

Dr. Méjico writes as a companion, not as an authority above pain. His reflections are grounded in prayer, shaped by humility, and infused with compassion. He walks beside the reader, reminding us that wherever we find ourselves in the grief process, raw, numb, angry, faithful, or unsure, we are not walking alone.

If you are holding this book, take your time. Let the words meet you where you are. Return to them as often as you need. Grief is not something we conquer. It is something we learn to live with, through contemplative prayer, through meaning-making, and in the presence of a God who does not leave.

This book is an invitation to that sacred companionship and to a joy that can only be found on the other side of being fully present with our grief and fully held by God.

Dr. Angie Cruz, LCSW
Founder, Loss y Luz 4 Kids
www.lossyluz4kids.com

Introduction: God, Give Me a Clean Heart

"Sometimes the healing hurts more than the wound."

—Anonymous

I had naively thought that my second book would be easier to write. You see, writing my first book was a difficult process for several reasons. I had not written a book before, and the subject matter I chose for my first book was challenging on many levels. It required deep introspection of my own spiritual development in response to difficult moments in my life and discussed social topics that have led to great amounts of division and pain throughout our country. Still, the process was cathartic and seemed to accomplish my intended outcome of helping others who were similarly struggling with the division and hate plaguing our world. A few months after publishing that book, I told myself, "The next book won't be as heavy. The process should be much smoother the second time around." My assessment was far from correct.

As you may know, God tends to speak to us in subtle yet powerful ways, and when we least expect. This time was no different. I had been praying for discernment on the topic of my next book and was having a difficult time determining what I would write next. Weeks had passed and while a few good ideas had crossed my mind, nothing in particular was stirring my soul. I knew that if I were to commit to starting and completing another book, I had to select a topic that I felt personally connected to, and would be helpful to the readers. I know that God does not always show up on my time, but he is always on time, so I trusted fully that when the moment was right, the topic would appear. I trusted that God would reveal the focus of my next book, if I was still and observant enough to hear him. I had underestimated, though, the circumstances in which he would appear.

During the fall semester of 2025, I was leading a meeting that included all the faculty and staff that work within the department I oversee. Each month, over thirty faculty and staff meet to discuss important updates related to our programs and the broader institution. Due to the myriad of courses to teach, community service obligations, and meeting schedules, it can be difficult to find a time that works for everyone, and when we do meet, time is often very tight, and the agenda is always very full. This meeting was no different. Before starting the meeting, I scanned the agenda one more time to prioritize the topics and determine where I would pivot in the agenda, if necessary. The week prior to the meeting was a difficult one for our country. Several acts of violence had plagued our country, and communities were more divided than ever. Communities were fractured and suffering, and our faculty, staff, and students were mourning several tragic losses that occurred at the hands of gun violence and political tension across our nation.

I start each of my meetings with the faculty and staff with what I call a "one-word check-in." In one word, each person shares how they are feeling in that very moment. The purpose of the check-in is to collect a sense of how the team is feeling and gather an overall baseline of the group's morale. As each faculty member shared their word, it was quickly apparent that there was a broad spectrum of feelings present in the room. Feelings of joy, contentment, anxiety, determination, anger, and frustration were shared. During the check-in, one of the team members arrived a little late to the meeting, just in time to hear a few of her colleagues share their one word. After the check-in, another faculty member delivered a devotion and opened the meeting in prayer.

After the prayer, I acknowledged the heaviness in the room, as well as the tragic events that had taken place just a few days before. The team seemed to be ready to move forward with the agenda. Some faculty took out their notebooks signaling they were ready to dive into the work. Then I asked the team if there were any comments related to the devotion or check-in. The faculty member that arrived late stated, "I guess I'm going to ask for you all to pray for me, because as I hear the words of some of my colleagues . . . well, I guess I'm not feeling joyful, or content at the moment. I'm not OK. I'm bothered by the events that occurred last week, and I'm angry, and I'm frustrated. I'm hurting and I don't feel very peaceful right now."

At that moment, I had to make a decision. You see, if you ever served in an administrator role, you know time with your entire team is precious and limited. I had planned to share a few very important updates and topics of discussion for the meeting, and I knew that if the conversation took longer than a few minutes, we most likely would not get through the entire agenda. I needed input from my team on urgent institutional matters and was feeling pressed to move on to the next item. But as I listened to the comments of the faculty member who had just shared her feelings related to the previous week's events, I realized she was not just upset, or angry, or frustrated . . . she was grieving.

Grief tends to do that. It appears suddenly and sometimes without warning. And when it does, it can derail the patterns and routines of individuals and communities. Elizabeth Gilbert once wrote, "Grief is a force of energy that cannot be controlled or predicted. It comes and goes on its own schedule. Grief does not obey your plans or wishes. . . . In that way, grief has a lot in common with love."[1] I could not agree more. In that moment, I realized that grief had shown up and taken hold of the meeting. I could press on with the agenda and ask the faculty to "park" that discussion to allow time to discuss other urgent topics, or I could choose to respond differently. If grief is in fact similar in its presentation to love, then we know that like love, we have to give space for grief. When we love someone, we know that sometimes we have to step back and give them their space to be with their feelings. We can't force our own thoughts, hopes, or desires on someone we love. We can only give them space and be present with them in the midst of that emotion until they determine they are ready to engage in a way that makes sense for them.

In that moment, I chose to leave the space open for the team to respond to our colleague. What followed was a powerful demonstration of the closeness of the team. In the minutes to follow, faculty and staff would share that they too were reeling from the previous week's events. Some shared that they were also broken from the violence that occurred throughout the country the previous week. Others shared that in those moments, they leaned in to their relationship with Christ, and that sustained them. Some said they processed their feelings with close family and friends. Others spoke with their pastors. Others stated that amid so much division, they still placed their hope in God's promise that he will "make all things new."

1. Gilbert, as cited in Youssef, "Elizabeth Gilbert Explains Grief."

I listened patiently and watched the team surround a grieving colleague with compassion and hope. After a few minutes, the faculty member thanked the team for their support. We continued with the meeting, and I still found the time to discuss the items on the agenda that were of highest priority. Following the meeting, a couple of faculty members texted me. They thanked me for allowing space to shift the meeting and allow time to comfort another colleague. They stated that I managed the meeting well and appreciated my leadership. Their feedback was very helpful, and I appreciated them taking the time to share their sentiments. But if I am honest, I struggled a little with the feedback. You see, my intention was not to "manage" the grief that suddenly took hold of the meeting. I was not trying to tamp out the pain or move on from the grieving process. I simply saw that one of our team members was hurting, and I wanted her to know that we saw her pain and that her wellness took priority over the action items of the meeting. I only wanted us to respond to our colleague's grief with compassion.

After the meeting, I went home and completed my evening routine of cooking dinner for the family and ironing my clothes for the next day. My daughter was finishing her homework, and my wife was planning for the next day's activities. After the family had gone to sleep, I sat down to pray and reflect upon the focus of this book. I had just finished watching the evening news. The stories of the news that week were filled with violence, political tension, contentious topics and divided perspectives. I was reeling a bit from the brief but concentrated exposure to the brokenness of the world during the newscast and was also reflecting on the dynamics of the team meeting that had occurred just a few hours before. I could not quite place what I was feeling. There was a heaviness in my heart, mixed with a feeling of emotional fatigue. There was a somberness hanging over me that I could not quite shake, and as I reached for my Bible to engage in my centering exercises, I took a deep breath and opened the book of Psalms, and Ps 51:1–15 (NLT) emerged. Here are the verses I read that evening.

> Have mercy on me, O God,
>   because of your unfailing love.
> Because of your great compassion,
>   blot out the stain of my sins.
> Wash me clean from my guilt.
>   Purify me from my sin.
> For I recognize my rebellion;
>   it haunts me day and night.

Against you, and you alone, have I sinned;
  I have done what is evil in your sight.
You will be proved right in what you say,
  and your judgment against me is just.
For I was born a sinner—
  yes, from the moment my mother conceived me.
But you desire honesty from the womb,
  teaching me wisdom even there.
Purify me from my sins, and I will be clean;
  wash me, and I will be whiter than snow.
Oh, give me back my joy again;
  you have broken me—
  now let me rejoice.
Don't keep looking at my sins.
  Remove the stain of my guilt.
Create in me a clean heart, O God.
  Renew a loyal spirit within me.
Do not banish me from your presence,
  and don't take your Holy Spirit from me.
Restore to me the joy of your salvation,
  and make me willing to obey you.
Then I will teach your ways to rebels,
  and they will return to you.

I sat with the word for a moment and quietly whispered, "God, give me a clean heart." It may sound odd to say this, but as I whispered those words, I felt a little fear entering my heart. When I'm speaking to God, particularly when I'm asking for his guidance or support with something I'm going through, I don't take that lightly. When I heard the words leave my mouth, I knew that I was not only asking for me to be at peace in that moment—I was asking to be cleansed. Finding peace and being cleansed are both complex and challenging processes.

When David wrote Ps 51, he was paralyzed by a deep sense of debilitating grief. David had committed adultery and even ordered the husband of the woman he was cheating with to be murdered. David had succumbed to his own carnal urges and used his power as king to harm others. He had abandoned his relationship with God in exchange for lust and power. God sent the prophet Nathan to call David out on the sins he committed. When confronted with his sins, David was consumed with guilt and shame. He grieved the harm he had done to others and was physically and emotionally unwell. He was hurting emotionally and spiritually, and his grief became too much for him to bear. He asked God to "blot out the stains" of his sins and to have mercy on him. David feels physically and spiritually dirty from the sins he committed. You can see the guilt and shame David was battling with in the lines of his Scripture: "For I recognize my rebellion; it haunts me day and night. . . . Do not banish me from your presence. Make me willing to obey you." David could not shake the shame of his sins. They haunted him day and night and constantly weighed on his thoughts. He feels as though he's the sum of the worst thing he has done. He's effectively saying, "I am my sins, and I am ashamed of myself. Please God, don't turn your back on me. I am unworthy, and I am so sorry for the harm I've done to others. I'm sorry for abusing my power. I'm sorry for giving in to lust and greed. God, don't give up on me. God, forgive my sins. Wash away my unholiness. Give me a clean heart, so that I can continue to bring others to you."

Reader, please sit with that for a moment. Picture a king, adorned in garments of fine linens and gold on his knees, weeping and pleading with God. Imagine the extreme humility and shame it took for David—who holds all power in the earthly sense to do as he pleases—to surrender himself to God. David was not OK when he wrote Ps 51. He was hurting and must have felt powerless before God. He had reached a point when the hurting was too much for him.

Grief took hold of David and disrupted the patterns of his life. It turned him upside down emotionally to the point where David pleads with God to give him a clean heart. This cleansing was not born from peace and serenity. It was born from deep pain, sorrow, and regret. Psalm 51 is a message of repentance, rooted in paralyzing grief. For David to be cleansed, he had to confront his grief. He had to reflect on the emotions that were eating him alive, as well as the source of that grief that stemmed from his own brokenness as a person. He could not be cleansed without doing the tough work of first addressing his grief.

So, when I heard myself asking God to give me a clean heart, I grew nervous. I was worried about what that would look like for me. Artists whose medium is clay teach us that when you shape clay into an object, it will only hold its form temporarily. Even after the clay has been formed, it's still weak and incapable of fulfilling its intended purpose. If you form a pot out of clay, it may look like a pot but it's still incomplete and incapable of fulfilling its purpose. If you don't place the clay pot into an oven, it will simply return to the formless matter it was before the sculptor created it.

When the clay pot enters the oven, it is exposed to intense heat and pressure. The flames burn away the impurities until what emerges from the oven is an object that can now be used as the potter intended. It is not until the clay pot has survived its trial by fire that it can hold water to sustain life, oils to sooth wounds or anoint kings, or store food to last the bitter winter months. The pot must face the roaring flames, heat, and intense pressure to be purified. After centering on Ps 51 that evening, I realized God revealed to me the focus of this book. He was calling me to share with you the grief I have experienced in my life, and to provide examples of how he has been present in my own process of walking with grief. You see, reader? I thought this book would be easier to write. God had other plans.

Walking with grief, or what is sometimes referred to by counselors as grief work, is a trial by fire. The initial trauma we experience, the source of our grief, is the initial process of formation. We are changed by the tragic event, but if we don't surrender to the painful process of acknowledging our grief, we stay in the same formless state where grief found us. Fr. Greg Boyle says, "We want to make sure that grief doesn't leave you where it found you. . . . We ought not to settle for sadness."[2] But what can grief possibly teach us? If we ought not to settle for sadness, then what am I hoping to gain? What does grief have to offer us that "forms" us into something stronger, and aligned with a purpose? How can you honestly say that grief work is "worth it" when I am consumed by such pain and sorrow? I can't even get out of bed in the morning, and the hurting is too much. How can you tell me that I can ever recover from this type of pain? During the process of centering on Ps 51, it suddenly became evident to me that the feeling I was trying to identify before I had started centering that evening was grief. Like my faculty, I too was feeling the weight of grief, and I was asking God to help me process the intense feelings of loss and frustration during my grief. I asked God to cleanse my heart and grant me peace. What I was asking for, in essence, was for the courage to see and understand my grief more deeply, and to examine where I have seen and experienced God in the process of walking with grief. Some of you may have recently experienced intense grief. Others of you may still be walking with grief to this day. In either case, you may find this book helpful.

It would be arrogant and insensitive for me to say that grief is a gift, considering the pain you might be feeling from a significant loss, but what I can say is that after years of walking with grief that has presented itself

2. Boyle, *Tattoos on the Heart*, 55.

in various forms throughout my life, I can see that walking with my grief has blessed me. I don't necessarily think that grief in and of itself is the gift, but from a spiritual perspective, the process of surrendering myself to God in my moments of grief has blessed me. It's a bridge that provides an opportunity to understand ourselves and our relationship with God more intimately. It's brought me closer to God and others. It's also given me purpose. We never fully abandon feelings of grief; rather, we learn to make space for it in our lives. Grief works a spiritual muscle that we often have neglected and expands our hearts. It helps us love more deeply and provides us with a new understanding and appreciation for joy. The longer we work through our grief in the presence of God, we become aware of the fact that grief eventually releases its grip on us, and instead of a punisher, grief becomes a teacher. Fr. Richard Rohr wrote, "The process of walking with grief is characterized by learning to carry a kind of 'bright sadness, sober happiness or luminous darkness.' It is living with the simultaneous existence of deep suffering and intense joy."[3] Please hear me when I say that the purpose of this book is not to teach you how to move past your grief. I am not proposing that you should just "get over it" or stop feeling sad; rather, this book is intended to provide you with a few tools that I have gained over the years that have helped me understand and walk with my grief more deeply.

The lessons I have included in this book come from years of practicing contemplative prayer and running to God during deep periods of grief. Contemplative prayer is a form of meditation that leads a person into a deep and intimate conversation with God. When it comes to grief work, contemplative prayer is like stepping into an oven, where you are subjected to the heat and pressures of the emotions that often accompany loss, and as you walk with your feelings of sadness, anger, denial, etc., the impurities are burned away. You strive to look beyond the human emotions and social expectations that pressure you to say things like "I'm fine" or succumb to the expectation that "it's time to move on." Contemplative prayer invites you to stand next to your grief and gaze into a spiritual mirror that reflects the pain you are feeling, but also the love you hold in your heart, as you examine how the sudden end of a relationship has impacted you emotionally, physically, and spiritually. What remains is God's promise to us, that he will be with us in every one of life's events, including our grief. There are many forms of contemplative prayer, like Centering Prayer, the Lectio Divina, the

3. Rohr, *Falling Upward*, 75.

Jesus Prayer, and the Daily Examen, and each of these practices herald back to ancient mystics from as far back as the third century. If you would like to learn more about contemplative prayer, please refer to my first book, *The Way of Love: Biblical Reflections on Oneness, Hope, and Extravagant Love in Divided Times*. I explain the process of contemplative prayer more in that book as it relates to difficult social topics such as race, class, ethnicity, and politics.

This book will focus on how I came to discover contemplative prayer, and how it helped me cope with intense losses in my life and strengthen my relationship with God. It is a guide that is intended to help you establish your own practice of contemplative prayer in your daily routine in the hope that you, too, will be transformed by the word of God, and know him in the way that I have come to know him. Throughout this book, you will hear personal stories of times I have grieved, and the revelations God shared with me during my moments of contemplative prayer.

Over the course of this book, I will explain various forms of contemplative prayer in the context of grief work and will guide you through several spiritual exercises that you can then use to help you in your own walk with grief. This book will highlight the Jesus Prayer, Centering Prayer, the Lectio Divina, and the Daily Examen. Each of these forms of contemplative prayer are unique in their own right, yet similar in the sense that each draws you into a very close and personal encounter with God. Over the course of the day, I may use one or all these forms of contemplative prayer, depending on what I am experiencing that day. I encourage you to choose at least one and commit to integrating it into your own grief work for at least thirty days and reflect upon the changes you experience in your own life. After ten years of practicing contemplative prayer, I can honestly say that it has fundamentally changed my walk with Christ, and my relationship with others. It also helped me walk with my own grief during very difficult times.

In my first book, I discussed the impact of engaging with contemplative practices, but I did not share the origin of my introduction to contemplative prayer. I did not discover contemplative prayer until 2015, when I was thirty-four years old. Before that time, I mostly tried to manage difficult seasons of heavy loss as most people do. I lived in denial that my grief was as bad as it was or told people I was "fine" when I really wasn't. I tried to push the sadness that would sometimes consume me from my mind with work or school, telling myself I was "too busy to grieve right now" or even tried to numb the pain with whatever substance I thought could do the trick. Those were the impurities. In the back of my mind, I had always known that God was calling me to address my grief. He was inviting me to sit with him and talk about the ways my heart was broken, and acknowledge that my coping skills, or lack thereof, were only making me more unwell. But a part of me feared this conversation and was unsure of how to go about exploring my grief in a faith-integrated way.

Then, in 2015, I was introduced to a type of grief I had not known. I will explain more about that loss in a subsequent chapter of this book, but what I will say here is that the season of grief that struck me in 2015 turned my world upside down. I could not smile. I could not laugh. I did not want to eat. I could not sleep through the night without waking up in a panic, or in tears. I faced bouts of weeping that would suddenly overwhelm me without warning, and my heart was so angry with the entire world. It was an anger I had never felt before, and it felt like a pure and unfiltered rage burning in my heart that could not be extinguished. I was consumed by my grief every moment of every day until I contacted a former professor of mine whom I respected deeply. He taught me courses in counseling and social justice during my master's and doctoral programs and was a brilliant and faith-based philosopher and mystic. After sitting down with him for many talks, which a therapist would have described as "sessions," he helped me understand my feelings more deeply and identified the source of my brokenness as grief. He also introduced me to contemplative prayer. It is those insights that I have gained over the past ten years, after standing in the flames of my grief that I have shared in this book.

Throughout the book, you will notice I address you directly as "reader." My intent is to walk with you in your grief as you read this book. My intent is to share what I have learned as a counselor and helping professional assisting others in managing their grief and share with you how I eventually found joy and peace in the midst of my own intense suffering. My goal is not to tell you how to grieve or when you should stop grieving, but rather to demonstrate that once we commit to the trial by fire, our hearts come out of the oven stronger and purer in our love for ourselves, others, and God. I wish to provide you with a few tools that might help you endure the fire that is consuming you, so that you may walk with your grief in a manner that no longer takes hold of you, but may actually help you love more deeply, and experience joy more intensely even in the presence of deep loss. As you read this book, you will most likely find your heart returning to moments when you were first introduced to intense grief. You may experience painful memories and emotions that you thought you had forgotten. That's OK and is a natural part of grief work. I would encourage you to lean in to those feelings and examine their source more closely and then talk to God about those feelings. Put the book down in those moments, pray, and then revisit the content. Remember that even when you feel as though the hurting is too much, God is forever present in the midst of your sorrow, and his heart is breaking too.

1

When the Hurting Is Too Much

"Grief does not obey your plans, or your wishes. Grief will do whatever it wants to you, whenever it wants to. In that regard, grief has a lot in common with love."
—Elizabeth Gilbert

One of the amazing things about teaching in higher education is the innate opportunity to shape the lives of students studying in a university setting. Each year, I teach courses that vary in student enrollment and content focus. Some of my classes are as small as eight students, and others are much larger with over one hundred students enrolled. I have had the privilege of teaching first-time freshmen who are just starting their journeys of earning their bachelor's degree, as well as master's and doctoral students who are returning to school after years of serving in their chosen profession. Each group of students is distinctively different from the other and I am always amazed at the ways God weaves his way through the interactions between me and my students each semester.

In the spring semester of 2025, I was scheduled to teach a group of pre-nursing and speech pathology students. Part of the prerequisites required to apply for the nursing program are for students to take a psychology course titled "Lifespan Development for Health Professionals." Classes tend to be smaller in the fall, with about forty-five students enrolled, but in the spring, class sizes are much larger, usually around sixty-five students to as many as one hundred students enrolled in one section. I love teaching this course because so many of the students are new to the university by way of first-time enrollment as a freshman, or as a new transfer student, just joining the university. I have taught the class many times before over the years and am very comfortable with the content. The course takes students through the stages of human development from inception to death, and over the years of teaching the course, I added a section on grief to provide tools for future nurses and speech pathologists to help their clients manage the grieving process after the loss of a loved one.

As a university professor, I hear lots of reasons from students as to why they miss class, or why their academic performance begins to decline. "I have a doctor's appointment. My alarm didn't go off. My car broke down. I was in an accident. I felt ill. I'm not a morning person. My dog passed away. I needed a mental health day" are frequent emails that cross my desk. Sometimes students send pictures of doctor's notes, lab test results, and dented and scratched bumpers as evidence of the request to excuse their absences. After years of teaching, if you are not careful, one can easily begin to dismiss the majority of reasons students miss class or an assignment and become calloused in your response. In each of these cases, I try to work with the students to bring them back on track so they can successfully complete the course, though results may vary.

One particular semester I was teaching Lifespan Development with sixty-two pre-nursing and speech pathology students. The majority of students tend to start the semester off strong, with consistent attendance and assignments submitted on time. As the semester progresses, usually about week five or six into the fourteen-week course, attendance sporadically drops off with assignments also being missed for a small group of students. This semester I noticed that one particular student stood out. Her attendance and exam scores were perfect every week, and her thoughts shared in her assignments were insightful and demonstrated a passion for the course content. Suddenly, at about week five, the student was absent from class. I thought it was odd, but realized things happen and didn't think too much of it. Then she missed an assignment. Over the next couple of weeks, I noticed that she did not attend one class or submit any other work. Her grade was now in jeopardy, and I was concerned with the dramatic and sudden decline of her studies due to the excellent work she had completed at the beginning of the semester. I reached out to the student via email to check in with her and shared that I had noticed a sudden drop in attendance and assignment submissions. I asked her if we might be able to connect before or after the next class to discuss her performance. A week had passed, and I still hadn't heard anything from the student.

One afternoon in between teaching classes and meetings, I darted to my office to respond to a few emails. I was in a rush since I was scheduled to teach another class within the hour. I needed to respond to students and colleagues as quickly as possible and still prepare for my next class. My fingers swept gingerly across the keyboard. I scanned the emails quickly and carefully crafted my responses so as to respond as concisely and efficiently as possible. As I moved through my inbox at a rapid pace, I saw the name of the student whom I had reached out to. The email read:

> Dear Dr. Méjico,
>
> I wanted to reach out before we talk after class on Wednesday. I take full responsibility for my absences and for how much I've fallen behind. I know how important it is to show up and stay on top of schoolwork, and I know I've let that slip this semester. I'm really sorry I didn't email you sooner or explain what was going on.
>
> The truth is, my dad suddenly passed away during the first few weeks of the semester, and ever since then, I've been struggling a lot. I've been feeling really depressed, and some days it's hard for me to even get out of bed, let alone make it to class. I've never felt this way before, and it's honestly been really hard to deal with. This isn't like me at all and I usually care so much about my education and being responsible, but lately I just feel lost.
>
> I know these aren't excuses, and I'm not trying to avoid taking accountability. I just wanted to be honest with you, because I know I might not be able to say all of this out loud without getting emotional. I should've reached out sooner, but I didn't know how to handle what I was going through, and I've been stuck in that mindset for a while now.
>
> Thank you for taking the time to read this. I really appreciate your understanding, and I'm trying my best to pull myself out of this and get back on track.
>
> Sincerely,
> [Student]

I paused for a moment, and without realizing it, my hands covered my mouth as my elbows rested on the top of my desk. All I could do was stare at the screen for a couple of minutes as my mind attempted to process what I had just read. The typical rush of the administrator's pace of work that had previously consumed me came to a screeching halt. I shook my head in disbelief and closed my eyes. Over the years of teaching courses, students had shared losses with me before, mostly grandparents, aunts, or uncles. But this email had a profound effect on me for several reasons. One of which is because this student just shared with me a sudden and painful loss she had experienced. I can only imagine how difficult it was for her to write this message and the paralyzing grief she was feeling at that moment. The second reason this email impacted me so deeply is that I am a father of a fifteen-year-old daughter. I was reading the email from the lens of a professor, and the lens of a father.

As I read the email again, a few words touched my heart deeply and briefly brought me to a moment of tears. I've italicized those words in the email below, so you can see where my heart was touched that afternoon. I'd ask you this time to only read the italicized words in the letter below.

> Dear Dr. Méjico,
>
> I wanted to reach out before we talk after class on Wednesday. I take full responsibility for my absences and for how much I've fallen behind. I know how important it is to show up and stay on top of schoolwork, and I know I've let that slip this semester. I'm really sorry I didn't email you sooner or explain what was going on.
>
> The truth is, *my dad suddenly passed away* during the first few weeks of the semester, and ever since then, *I've been struggling a lot*. I've been feeling really depressed, and some days *it's hard for me to even get out of bed*, let alone make it to class. *I've never felt this way before*, and it's honestly been really hard to deal with. This isn't like me at all and I usually care so much about my education and being responsible, but lately I just feel lost.
>
> I know these aren't excuses, and I'm not trying to avoid taking accountability. I just wanted to be honest with you, because I know I might not be able to say all of this out loud without getting emotional. I should've reached out sooner, but I didn't know how to handle what I was going through, and *I've been stuck* in that mindset for a while now.
>
> Thank you for taking the time to read this. I really appreciate your understanding, and *I'm trying my best* to pull myself out of this and get back on track.
>
> Sincerely,
> [Student]

Tears welled up in my eyes and the lump in my throat made it difficult to swallow. If you were to ask someone to share their greatest fear, you might be surprised to learn that it's a fear that they tend to never discuss out loud, not even with the people closest to them. It's the fear that we hold deeply in the marrow of our being and keep it locked away from others so as to avoid them seeing it. We don't want them to know that we carry a fear that is so bothersome to us that we dare not even speak of it at the risk of it coming true. I'm going to share my greatest fear with you now. It is the fear that I carry deep in my heart and never speak of openly. Not even to my family or friends. My greatest fear is that I will die before I've had the chance to see my daughter marry or have a family. My fear is that I will pass suddenly and unexpectedly, and my daughter will be in her late teens or early twenties, and that my passing will impact her profoundly and negatively change the trajectory of her life. I am not scared of dying. I realize it is a part of life and that it's something that I will face eventually. Rather, my fear is that I will die at a time when my daughter needs me the most, and that absence will hurt her deeply and send her down a path of grief that she would become lost in for years to come and in the prime years of her life.

As I read the email, the words I've italicized in the script above spoke to my greatest fear. That I will pass away suddenly and unexpectedly, and that my daughter would find herself in the very same paralyzing grief as this student. That my daughter would be hurting, depressed, and new to experiencing this level of grief, and that she would be so stricken by sadness that she cannot rise from bed or function. That she would be carrying so much pain that she could not even speak of the grief she was feeling out of fear of completely collapsing. My heart was moved by this email. I did not just feel bad for the student. That would have been me being sympathetic for her situation. This was something different. My heart was hurting for this student. Scripture tells us that in the Old Testament, God felt compassion for his people, and in the New Testament, Jesus was "moved by compassion" when interacting with people who had encountered great suffering (Matt 14:14 ESV). What I felt in that moment was compassion towards this student. I will elaborate on the differences in a subsequent chapter, but in that moment, I paused and said a prayer for the student and her father and responded to her email.

> [Student],
>
> My heart is hurting for you. I'm so very sorry that you have lost your father. I am a father, and my daughter is fifteen years old. I can only imagine what you are going through. I am here and want to help. Let's find a time when you feel comfortable enough

to talk. Please don't worry about the course. We'll get that figured out. Let's just focus on what you need during this difficult time. I am praying for you and your father.

My deepest sympathies,
Dr. Méjico

The next week, after class, students scurried from the classroom. A few stayed behind to ask questions about the course, or comment on the lecture. I noticed that the student who had been communicating with me via email was waiting patiently in the back of the room. She waited for the other students to finish their questions and leave the classroom. She and I stood near the podium in the large empty lecture hall. I looked at her, and she looked at me. Her eyes began to water. She said nothing. Thick tears began to roll down her cheeks. I looked back at her, tears now forming in my own eyes. I said, "I'm so sorry. I'm so sorry you are experiencing this."

The student sobbed quietly and said, "It just hurts so much. I don't know what to do. Sometimes I can't believe he's gone. I don't want to think that he's never coming back. The hurting is too much. I miss him so much."

"You must have loved your father very much," I said to her.

She gently nodded her chin and said, "I wanted him to see me graduate. He never went to college." As she wept, her body began to shake. She looked as though she would collapse from the weight of her grief.

I'll never forget those words the student said to me. "The hurting is too much." Her response broke my heart again. It is exactly the position I fear leaving my daughter in. Her pain was so evident, and at that moment, her brokenness was so deep. I asked the student if I could give her a hug. It's not something that I typically do with students, but I could see the pain she was feeling, and my heart was moved by compassion. She nodded her head, and I hugged the student briefly as she wept. The student slowly stopped weeping, and I asked her if she was a believer. She nodded her head again, wiping away her tears, and I asked if she would be comfortable with me praying for her and her father. She responded, "I'd like that."

We prayed together in the classroom and then just sat and talked for a few minutes. After listening to the student for a few moments, it became apparent why she loved her father so much. He emigrated from Mexico for a better life and owned a landscaping business. He awoke at 4 a.m. every day to mow lawns, repair sprinklers, and trim trees. He sacrificed everything for his family and always told his daughter that he wanted to see her graduate from college, because he had never had the chance to attend school past the eighth grade. He had a preexisting heart condition that was rarely, if ever, treated because he could not take off work and lose a day's income to go to the community health clinic. He had paid his daughter's tuition each semester with his own blood and sweat and always told her that whatever she needed for school, he would cover even if he had to work harder. She was the first in her family to attend college and wanted to make her father proud. Her story is a common one for many students with immigrant parents who labor with their hands every day to carve out a better path for their children, but the sacrifices her father made demonstrated his profound love for her. She saw how much her father loved her every day as the work truck pulled out of the driveway for a long day laboring in the blazing sun or bitter cold so that he would see the day she crossed the stage in her regalia, holding her diploma. That vision was suddenly gone, and the student was left feeling lost and missing her father immensely.

I asked her if I could share a few resources available to her on campus to assist her in completing the semester. She agreed, and over the next few minutes, we talked about a few resources on campus, and I offered to connect her to them personally. She mentioned that she was also connected with a counselor outside of the university. We made plans for the remaining weeks of the course, and eventually she ended up completing the course successfully. I will never forget, though, that deep and unexpected connection to grief that occurred that semester. It was an exchange that was deeper than student and professor, or father and daughter. It was a moment where two individuals sat in a space of deep pain with no expectation other than to be present with one another. Words could not fix this grief. A hug could not heal the wound. But the fact that someone was willing to sit with another person in a very vulnerable and difficult moment created a brief pause where the weight of the grief was not carried by the student alone.

I think the type of interaction I shared with the student after class captures the focus of this book—to talk about what it's like to manage a grief that is so heavy, so deep, and so paralyzing that, like the student, we reach a point where "the hurting is too much." I, like you, have experienced moments of intense grief in my life. Each source or season of grief was different and grabbed ahold of me in its own way. And in each of those cases, there were moments where I felt the hurting was too much. There were moments where grief stole my breath and froze my legs. It held me captive in my bed for days and kept me from eating or smiling. It's the grief that caused me to briefly step away from my career in child welfare, and in a way, it's the same grief that brought me back to my walk with Jesus. If that grief is what has led you to pick up this book, I want to tell you I'm sorry for what you are experiencing, and that I hope this book is helpful to you. In Matt 5:4 (NLV) Jesus tells us, "Blessed are those who mourn, for they shall be comforted." The Scripture suggests that God sees our grief, is present in our mourning, responds to it with an extravagant love, and eventually, leads us to a place of deep and boundless peace that releases us from grief's suffocating grip. I cannot tell you what that process looks like for you, since God always meets us where we are, but I can share with you what that process looked like for me.

This book is for those who mourn. For those who feel so consumed by their grief that it hurts to sleep in the bed they once shared with their partner or spouse. It's for the person who plays the last voicemail from their loved one who has passed, over and over, just to hear their voice one more time. It's for the child that is lost and emotionally numb after losing a parent to cancer, or suicide, or divorce. It is for the parent who is grappling with understanding why their child passed before they did. It is for the person who can still hear the laugh and feel the hug of the person they miss deeply. This book shares my experiences walking with grief through the spiritual guidance of my mentors, and from God's revelations to me during moments of engaging in contemplative prayer. If you feel lost in the midst of your grief, I pray that some of the insights I share in this book are of use to you, and that you might find some peace within yourself, and in your relationship with God. The hurting at times will feel like it's too much. But I can attest to the fact that God has delivered me from grief's hold and led me to green pastures and peaceful streams. The grief is too much for us to carry alone, but it is never too much for God.

A good place to begin processing our grief is to first examine what grief is. Many of us have an idea of grief's definition, but there are actually multiple definitions of grief. How we experience and manage grief has a lot to do with how we define it. If we are unaware of what grief is, we may not fully realize or understand what we are feeling and therefore will not know how to confront it. I would like to present several definitions of grief, so that you might be able to explore its meaning a bit more and perhaps connect to your own feelings and thoughts more deeply.

In their book *Thirty-Five Techniques Every Counselor Should Know*, Bradley Erford et al. define grief as a "keen mental suffering or distress over affliction or loss; sharp sorrow; or painful regret."[1] This definition is fine for basic purposes, but if you have ever experienced grief, I think you might agree that the feelings that grab hold of you while grieving are far more complex than what this definition offers. The definition fails to capture the complexity of emotions that follow us for months or years after we experience a painful loss in our lives. It also neglects to mention that our grief changes with time.

In the *APA Dictionary of Psychology*, the American Psychological Association defines grief as "the anguish experienced after significant loss, usually the death of a beloved person. Grief is often distinguished from bereavement and mourning."[2] This definition is better. It helps separate grief from bereavement and mourning, which is more focused on the feelings of sadness after a loss, most associated with death. This definition touches on the depth of loss felt using the word "anguish." The Latin root of "anguish" is *angustus*, which can mean "narrow" or "difficult." From the French root word of *angoisse*, it can mean "distress." You may have experienced grief similar to this definition, where the sadness, difficulty in functioning, and distress in your innermost being is suddenly activated and takes hold of you forcefully and suddenly.

Finally, in Dr. Brené Brown's book *Atlas of the Heart*, grief is defined as "the process of adapting to a group of emotions and experiences that accompany events that result in a personal or collective loss or create a sense of feeling lost or longing."[3] I find this definition to be the most helpful when helping others walk with their grief. It better captures what I saw in the student who lost her father. This definition doesn't settle for the feelings that follow after a significant loss; rather, it explains grief as a process that involves several complex emotions that all exist simultaneously. The process involves us trying to find new ways to adapt to those feelings, and what I appreciate most about this definition is that it does not say those feelings ever go away completely.

Dr. Brown's definition also distinguishes between individual and collective grief. That is important. In the introduction of this book, I noted that as a team, my faculty (me included) were collectively mourning the week of violence we had experienced in our country leading up to the meeting. I also discussed the individual grief that faculty member was attempting

1. Erford et al., *Thirty-Five Techniques*, 180.
2. American Psychological Association, "Grief."
3. Brown, *Atlas of the Heart*, 113.

to manage as she reflected on her own personal feelings. When those two elements of grief, the collective and the individual, collided within me that evening in prayer, it was enough for me to hear the Holy Spirit speaking to me to respond to that grief by writing this book. I'd ask you to pause for a moment and consider why you are hurting. Are you hurting in response to social events that are plaguing our society? Are you hurting from a deep personal and individual loss? Perhaps it's both. Grief doesn't fit into a nice, neat box. We can grieve individually when someone we love dies, and then find ourselves grieving collectively at their funeral, surrounded by hundreds of people who loved that person too. Sometimes, reflecting on how you are grieving, and who may also be grieving with you, helps to understand the source of our grief better.

From a spiritual perspective we can learn a lot from Scripture about grief. Grief is present in the first chapter of the Bible. In Genesis chapter 3, Adam and Eve eat the forbidden fruit in the garden of Eden. They broke their relationship with God in exchange for knowledge and pride. God enters the garden and asks Adam, "Where are you?" God is all-knowing and obviously knows where Adam and Eve are physically located in the garden. I don't think God is asking Adam where he is hiding physically. His question is a deeper question to Adam, Eve, and all of humanity. When God asks Adam, "Where are you?" he is effectively asking him, "Where are you hiding from me and our relationship? Where are you in relationship to me?" God is a heartbroken parent grieving the loss of his children. If you are a parent, imagine what it would feel like if your children were suddenly gone. God forbid. Imagine the pain he was feeling knowing the very beings he created rejected his love to pursue their own petty interests. I imagine God asking, "We used to be so close. You used to love me so deeply. Why did things change? Why did you stop loving me the same way I love you? I love you so much and you turned away from me. I'm hurting so deeply. Why did you leave me?" The Bible starts with God's grief and teaches us that sudden loss, and the pain that accompanies it, has been present since the dawn of man.

In their book *Beyond Homelessness: Christian Faith in a Culture of Displacement*, Steven Bouma-Prediger and Brian J. Walsh discuss the break from intimacy between Adam and Eve and God. They recount the story in Genesis chapter 3 with an emotional and poetic account of the fall of mankind in the biblical interlude within their book.[4]

4. Bouma-Prediger and Walsh, *Beyond Homelessness*, 29–37.

In this beautiful and heartbreaking account of the fall, God creates us in fear and wonderment (Ps 139:14). That means he created us in respect and awe. God is in awe of his children. He did not make us out of spite, or boredom, or to boast of his power. In this interlude he joyfully sings us into existence and is in awe of us. He walks with Adam and Eve in the garden in the cool evening breeze. He calls us "very good," even after everything he created beforehand was "good." We are the capstone of his creation, and his love literally provided us with a home and sense of belonging. When Adam and Eve abandoned God, he was heartbroken and stricken with grief. God's heartbreak was proportionate to his love. His pain matched the ecstasy he felt when he created us. So, grief enters God's heart, and the garden. Grief now becomes a part of the story of God's children.

In Scripture, the word "grief" was often described using the Greek word *lupe* or *lupeo* which describes being "swallowed up by sadness," and we see in Scripture that several biblical figures experienced deep, paralyzing individual and collective grief. Job grieved the loss of his children, material positions, and health. Naomi and Hannah experienced deep loss and paralyzing sorrow in their lives. King Herod grieved the decision he made to kill John the Baptist. King David grieved his moment of weakness consumed by lust and power. The rich man in the Gospel of Matthew grieved when Jesus told him that if we wanted to follow him with his whole heart, he'd need to abandon his wealth. The Israelites collectively grieved their enslavement and persecution at the hands of the pharaoh. Even Jesus wept when he saw Martha and Mary grieving the loss of his friend Lazarus, and he wept again in the garden of Gethsemane knowing he would soon be betrayed by his closest friends, falsely accused of crimes against the Roman Empire and Jewish law, and brutally tortured and murdered. What we take from Scripture is that grieving is a part of the human condition and that no one is immune to it. The question is not, "Will I experience grief?" Rather, "How will I walk with my grief, once I experience it?"

It is also important to note that grief needn't always be associated with death. Death is indeed a powerful and well-known source or catalyst of grief, but it is not the only reason people grieve. Other forms of grief may include:

1. A breakup or divorce
2. Chronic or terminal illness

3. Moving away from a familiar home, even if it's to seek a new and exciting opportunity
4. Promoting to a new position, and missing the job you once had
5. The loss of beloved pet
6. Promoting or graduating to elementary, middle, or high school
7. The transition of a child from one gender to another
8. Sudden and prolonged changes to routines that are out of our control, like the COVID-19 pandemic
9. A father and/or mother experiencing grief and joy when their child gets married
10. Immigrating from one's country of origin to another
11. When a close coworker moves/leaves the agency to pursue a new job opportunity or is even let go
12. When a dear friend suddenly ghosts you without warning

In each of these cases, grief may include a different mix of emotions, but the process of adapting to a new way of existing with these feelings remains. These events can move us from emotional stability to distress or uncertainty and disrupt the routine and sense of security in our lives. I would ask you to take a moment to reflect upon your source of grief. Does it align with the list above? Perhaps there are multiple sources of grief you are experiencing simultaneously. There may even be other sources of grief that you don't see on this list. That's OK. It's important to begin reflecting on what shifted you from your baseline level of functioning into this process of grief, and to determine if you are experiencing that grief alone, or within a community. That's a good place to begin processing your feelings and determining their origin.

As you explore the origin of your grief, you may find yourself hurting again or even experiencing new and painful feelings that you have not felt before. As I mentioned before, I did not always practice contemplative prayer. Before that, I struggled with identifying why I was grieving as well as naming the mix of feelings associated with my grief. As a result, I could not develop healthy ways of coping with that grief. If I felt tired, I took a nap, but I did not realize it was actually experiencing depression. If I ate junk food, it made me feel better, and I did not realize I was masking my feelings with a chemical response. If I was cranky or oppositional, I just thought I was having a bad day, not realizing I was consumed by the anger stage of my grief. Once you have labeled the source of your grief and the feelings that accompany it, you can begin to make a better plan for how to cope with those feelings and determine who to reach out to for support. Contemplative prayer helped me create a space for an open dialogue with God. While I usually use Scripture to guide my contemplation each day, during the midst of my heaviest days of grief, I would sometimes just sit in a quiet place, take deep, full breaths, and tell God how I was feeling. I would tell God about my anger or my sadness. I would name the source of loss that I was feeling, and I would ask God to help me name the feelings that were overwhelming me. I would reflect on my day searching for where God was present in my moments of grief.

The challenge with this approach is that the process of surrendering your grief to God during moments of contemplative prayer requires great humility. To give your grief to God is to acknowledge that we cannot carry grief on our own, at least not in a way that will keep us healthy or deepen our relationship with him. Surrendering to God requires us to first acknowledge we are hurting and then humble ourselves to the fact that we cannot carry this grief on our backs by ourselves. In moments of contemplation, I would often recite the Scripture from Matt 11:30 over and over: "My yoke is easy, and my burden is light." Jesus reminds us that through him, we find the spiritual rest from our grief. He is asking us to share that grief with him so that we might not burden ourselves with our own guilt, shame, anger, or sorrow. Nor are we to be burdened by the unrealistic expectations of society that often tell us to "get over it" or "move past our grief." Jesus doesn't tell us to move on. He asks us to move towards him and to take his yoke. We are not alone. Jesus wants to be a partner in your grief, and he provides us with the ability to lighten the burden of our sadness. In the next chapter I will share a very personal time when the hurting was just too much for me to bear, and I quickly realized that if I did not surrender my grief to God, my sorrow would consume me entirely.

2

In Search of the Yoke

"Grief, when it comes, is nothing like we expect it to be."

—Joan Didion

In the previous chapter we discussed the difficult but important first step of beginning our walk with grief. I shared different definitions of grief, and we explored the sources of grief that we may encounter throughout our lives. When we begin the journey of walking with grief, the steps are heavy and tiresome. Though I had experienced grief numerous times before the story I am about to share with you, I hadn't learned how to successfully name the source of my grief and the feelings that came with it—not until I discovered contemplative prayer. The story I am about to share was the catalyst for me discovering contemplative prayer, and I can honestly say, it saved my life. It led me closer in my walk with God, and it eventually helped me experience joy again more deeply than I had ever experienced in the past. But that journey of walking with God in the midst of my grief came from a very deep and painful place. Out of respect for my friend and his family, I have changed their names for the sake of this story, but the sequence of events occurred exactly as I have described.

In the summer of 1995, I joined the high school football team. The freshman team assembled for its first week of practices called hell week. Hell week was a grueling schedule of practices that actually ran for ten days (I don't know why they thought it was a good idea to call it a week). This included two practices each day, one in the morning and one in the evening. The coaches' job was to prepare the team for a challenging ten-week schedule of games, and hopefully a post-season schedule as well. In the middle of intense heat that surpassed one hundred degrees in the day, the team would run, lift weights, practice in full gear, and then run some more. It was a demanding schedule that tested the mental and physical endurance of every team member. It was also a time of anxiety for freshmen, since not many team members knew each other. You were being pushed to your physical and mental limits and were expected to form deep bonds with the players next to you.

During one scorching midday practice, the entire team was being disciplined for not working together as a unit. As we "bear crawled" across the dry, dusty field, gasping for air and praying for a water break, I heard the team member next to me grunting and wheezing underneath his helmet. He looked like he was going to keel over from exhaustion. We successfully made it to the end of the field and stood up to try and inhale as much of the hot and dusty air as we could, resting our hands on top of our helmets. The crown of the helmets was hot to the touch and sweat poured from the inside of our helmets onto our jerseys and the dead grass beneath our feet. I looked over to see a short, smaller team member gasping for air. He was small in stature but had a muscular build. His eyes were a piercing hazel, and his nose was small and pointy. I had played football since I was eight years old and was no stranger to the exhaustion he was feeling. I was feeling it too, but I had mentally prepared for the intensity of the workouts as I had completed hell week many times before. I looked over at him and said, "Have you played football before?"

"Nope," he said, still gasping for breath. The tip of his nose pointed straight up at the sky.

"You good, man?" I asked between my own gasping and wheezing.

"Nope," he said. "Wanna die."

We both chuckled knowing we felt the exact same way.

"Practice should be over soon. Just hang in there," I said. "They can't keep us here forever."

"They sure can," he said. "And now I shall hurl!" He yelled.

At that moment, he ripped the chin strap off the side of his helmet and yanked it off his head.

"Don't do that!" I yelled. "They're going to make us all run for taking off your helmet!"

"Don't care," he said.

He then began to heave violently. The entire team looked down the line at him and started yelling, "Don't do it! Don't you do it!" The coaches started yelling, "Who told you to take your helmet off? You better put that helmet on right now!"

After an atrocious sequence of heaving and coughing, he proceeded to vomit all over the grass in front of him. The hurling would not stop, and it didn't smell good at all. I couldn't believe the amount of substances leaving this guy's body. An audible "Ewwwww" bellowed from the team.

Another team member said, "I can't take it. I'm going to hurl."

A coach yelled, "Don't you dare throw up on my field!"

That didn't work. Another team member proceeded to vomit through his face mask, followed by another, and then another. Before long, at least six team members were vomiting in what seemed like a choreographed sequence all over the field.

The coaches couldn't do a thing but watch the madness ensue. The head coach said, "Well, I guess that's it. Practice is officially over, but you are all going to pay for this tomorrow. Dismissed!" The team began to scatter and make their way to the locker room. A few team members stayed back, still finishing desecrating the field with the contents of their breakfast. I looked over at my neighbor and said, "How do you feel now?"

"Still wanna die," he said.

We both started laughing. "I'm Antonio," I said.

"Mark," he said.

"Do you always hurl during practice?" I asked.

"Only when I eat steak and eggs for breakfast," he said, laughing.

"That's what that was!" I said. "Gross! Look man, maybe stick to something a little lighter for hell week," I joked.

"You think?" he said, giggling.

I'll never forget that giggle. It was a choppy, high-pitched "hehehe." As he laughed, he grinned ear to ear. He'd dip his chin down towards his chest and his shoulders moved up and down with every giggle in perfect sequence. His bright eyes peered at me, and he said, "What are you doing for dinner tonight?"

"How can you think about dinner right now?"

"It's what I do," he said in a mischievous tone, shrugging his shoulders with his palms pointing up at the sky.

That's how Mark and I met. What came of that awkward and gross interaction that day was a friendship that would last for twenty years. I was fourteen years old when I met Mark, and every day after that, we only grew closer. Over the next four years of high school, we grew so close that we considered each other brothers, and I loved him like a brother. Every summer during hell week, I would sleep at his parents' house since he lived closer to the school than me. I would swim at his house between practices, and we would go to the high school dances with our dates and other close friends. There were four of us in our crew that had grown close throughout high school. We considered ourselves brothers and laughed and fought as brothers would.

Mark was funny, passionate, engaging, and loyal, almost to a fault. He was a good-looking guy who always had girls chasing after him. He often spoke from the heart, and when he did, you could feel the sincerity in his voice. His giggle was contagious, and he had the ability to always find the good in people. It was annoying in fact. Whenever I would complain to him about how much I disliked someone, no matter how badly someone behaved or how rude they could be, he always ended the conversation with something like, "Yup. They're probably going through a lot right now." He always found a way to pull the grace from my heart and reset my expectations of people. I later realized his compassion for others came from a deep place of pain and emotional suffering that haunted him his entire life.

As funny and charismatic as Mark was around other people, when it was just me and him, he was very quiet and reserved. Sometimes when he came home from college to visit, he and I would sit on the porch outside his room at his parents' house late at night. We'd drink beer and listen to Bob Marley and the Wailers, Led Zeppelin, Jimi Hindrix, or Carlos Santana. He would become very quiet, and a wave of depression would flood over him, followed by intense anger. Sometimes when Mark drank, he would become violent and hostile towards others. He would want to fight with people in a bar or house party and took pride in his ability to fight men who were much larger than he was. Only I or another friend of ours could calm him down in these moments of rage.

Mark was born out of wedlock. His father was a university professor who had an inappropriate relationship with a student. His father abandoned the relationship immediately and his mother gave him up for adoption after he was born. Mark never met his biological mother or father. This was the source of his deep grief which was accompanied by feelings of abandonment, anger, and depression. During his sophomore year in high school, Mark began experimenting with substances to mask his feelings. He started drinking alcohol before school or between classes. He later began using cannabis and tobacco, and then moved on to harder drugs like cocaine, meth, mushrooms, Special K, and acid. He never exchanged one substance for another, rather he just added another substance to the rotation. At one point, his substance abuse became so severe that he was kicked out of college and had to move back home. Substance abuse was a part of his life, even during his first and second marriage and after the birth of his two children. He eventually quit using the harder drugs, but tobacco, cannabis, and alcohol abuse always remained present. He went to treatment and therapy for his addiction, and experienced brief moments of sobriety, only to relapse over and over again.

Mark was adopted by Mr. and Mrs. H. who were loving parents and were also very wealthy. He loved Mr. and Mrs. H deeply, but he could not shake the shame and rejection he felt from his biological parents. They lived in a mansion not far from the school that was built piece by piece from materials imported from Mexico. I'm not kidding. This was not just a big house. The property was terraced on six levels. It had its own garden on one level. A three-story house with a five-car garage and a woodworking shop above that. There was a pool above that, and a gazebo to take in the views of the entire city above that. Every stone, wood beam, tile, and window in the house was imported from Mexico. I used to joke with Mr. and Mrs. H and say their home looked like Scarface's mansion. Mrs. H referred to her home as the big Taco Bell restaurant on the block.

Mr. and Mrs. H ran a prominent law firm in the city and were well respected in the community. When Mr. and Mrs. H met, Mr. H was in seminary studying to be ordained as a Jesuit priest. Mrs. H was in formation to become a nun. They met, fell in love, married, and adopted five children, three boys and two girls. They took me in as their fourth son. I was always at their house studying, eating dinner with the family, hanging out with friends, or attending other functions they hosted.

They were staunch liberals and social justice warriors. They were activists who frequently hosted large fundraisers and dinners at their house that were attended by judges, politicians, and big business owners. Mr. H actually was arrested, tried, and served several years in Lompoc Federal Prison for speaking out against the United States government for their involvement in supporting the atrocities in El Salvador against the poor and the assassination of Archbishop Oscar Romero. They were also deeply connected to their faith. When I visited the family for dinner, which was a frequent occurrence, I noticed that before dinner, Mr. H would go into his home office. He would remain alone in his office for about an hour and then come down for dinner with the family. One evening, I quietly asked Mr. H why he went to his office every evening. I was about fifteen years old. He looked at me and smiled and said, "That's my time with God. It's when God talks to me, and I listen."

I responded to him, asking, "You mean like praying?"

He nodded his head and said, "It's like praying but even better. Some people call it centering. I'll teach you someday."

Mr. and Mrs. H introduced me to a lifestyle and concepts that I had not known before meeting them. When we had dinner as a family, Mr. H and Mrs. H would often serve steak, with potato salad or Caesar salad. The whole family would eat their steaks rare, and Mrs. H made the best potato salad I have ever eaten. The first time I had dinner at their house, Mr. H asked me how I liked my steak. I told him I liked my steak well done. It was the only way I had ever eaten it. He laughed and said, "You can have your steak any way you like it in this house, as long as it's rare." I learned to love my steak rare from that point on.

Before dinner, Mr. H would pray over the meal, and while we ate, he would ask us about school, sports, and our career aspirations. I was always amazed by how he would talk about the potential he saw in me. "You're going to make a difference in this world, Antonio. I know it. You have a kind heart and you're sincere." I was too young to fully understand what he meant at the time, but I know I always felt like Mr. H believed in me. He was a joker who laughed from the stomach and had the table laughing in tears as he told off-color jokes or shared stories of his time in seminary.

Frequently, Mr. and Mrs. H would invite me to the fundraisers and dinners they would host at their house. I didn't understand it at the time, but they were teaching me a new skill set related to economic class and networking. My family was not rich and before meeting Mark, I had never been exposed to this level of wealth. Prior to the guests arriving at the dinners and fundraisers at their house, Mrs. H. would brief me on who had RSVP'd for the event. She spent time sharing their educational background and profession with me. She reviewed the goal of the gathering, whether that was fundraising, introducing professionals to others in their network, or educating the group on current social topics and sharing ways attendees could get involved politically. She taught me that in these circles of networking, individuals will ask the same series of questions when she introduces me to them, questions like: Where do you go to school? Where will you be attending college? What are your career aspirations? What do your parents do? During the events she would introduce me to lawyers, politicians, entrepreneurs, activists, pastors and priests, and journalists. It was dizzying and it always seemed so awkward because I was a young person of color whose parents had barely made it into the middle class. Money was tight for our family, and I did not come from familial wealth or hold strong connections with people who were in positions of influence or power. The whole process was intimidating to me at first.

After the events ended and the guests had left, Mr. and Mrs. H would process the evening with me. They'd ask me what I thought about the guests, or the topics that were discussed and sometimes debated over dinner. They coached me on how to build my own personal network and in some cases, how to use their family name to gain opportunities for my education or career within their network. What I am trying to say is that Mr. and Mrs. H saw something in me that I did not see in myself. They not only adopted me into their family, but into their network of connections. They taught me about the language and culture of the upper class, and how to engage with prominent members of the community. They taught me that in these circles, the expectations of the group were that you would go to college, gain a career, and build your network. Money was not necessarily something to be saved or hoarded, rather, it was a tool to invest and gain more wealth. You tapped into your network to move up the social ladder and used the privilege you were born with or gained in life to help others who did not have the same opportunities. They helped shape my understanding of power dynamics, economic injustices, oppression, marginalization, equity, and social justice, all the while allowing me to be myself, develop my own thoughts and opinions, and make the mistakes that a typical teenager would make.

Mr. and Mrs. H would do anything for their children. They made sure that each one of them received the best education and healthcare from a young age. They kept them involved in sports and other extracurricular activities, always kept them safe, and constantly expressed to them that they were loved immensely. The second one of them struggled, they would seek the best support to help them manage the challenges they were facing. They wanted to provide their children with the opportunities they most likely would not have had if they had not been adopted. Despite these efforts and the seemingly endless financial resources, their family was not immune from its own trauma. Over the years, Mr. and Mrs. H would experience several painful moments of grief.

One of their sons battled severe depression, substance abuse, and schizophrenia. Despite their best efforts and after years of therapy, emotional and financial support, he eventually became homeless and passed away from a drug overdose in front of a grocery store less than two miles from their house. Mr. H never got to teach me about centering prayer. He passed suddenly and unexpectedly from a botched medical procedure during my first year in college that shook the core of the family and the community. His funeral was attended by over six hundred guests. These losses impacted me greatly as I considered myself part of the family. I inherited a part of their grief in these deep and painful moments that I still carry to this day. But as I was experiencing these painful moments, I had not yet learned how to define or manage my grief in healthy ways. So, I tried to push through my grief as most people do. I told myself I was fine and tried to distract myself with work, or food, or substances to manage the feelings I could not define, and they were consuming me.

As I stated, Mark also struggled in his own significant ways, and this broke his parents' hearts. It broke mine too. I stayed close to Mark through his years of substance abuse and depression. He and I would go on fishing trips with our friends; I was a groomsman at both his weddings. We'd go hiking, or to the shooting range. Sometimes, in the evenings, we roasted chicken over an open fire, drank a few beers, and laughed and joked about our high school days. We would then go inside and watch classic movies together. We'd sit quietly in front of the television eating chicken and French fries and chat about life until he eventually fell asleep in front of the TV due to the large quantity of alcohol he consumed. He was included in all my family events. He came to visit my daughter in the hospital after she was born, and I still remember the first time he held her in his arms after we brought her home. He held her gently, cradling her head in the bend of his elbow, and smiled at her warmly. He said to her, "You're so lucky to have a dad that loves you. You don't know how much he loves you." My eyes watered because I knew he was speaking from a place of deep sorrow and rejection from his biological parents. Life for Mark was difficult, but our friendship was strong, and things were "fine" in a sense for nearly two decades, until they weren't.

On the morning of February 16, 2015, I was getting ready to go golfing with a few of my close friends. I was in my upstairs bedroom putting on my shoes when the phone rang. I picked up the phone to hear one of Mark's sisters on the line. "Antonio," she said in a whimper. "Mark is dead." I could not process what I was hearing. I sat frozen on the bed, one shoe still on the ground.

"What did you just say?" I said in shock. I remember my heart was pounding and my palms immediately began to sweat. My breathing became rapid, and my vision began to blur.

"He's dead," she said. She then began to sob heavily on the phone.

"Mark. Our Mark . . . is dead? That's not funny, Maria," I responded in disbelief. "Whatever you're doing right now, it's not f—ing funny!" In my heart I knew she was not joking, but my mind could not understand the words she was telling me. I simply could not believe what I was hearing.

"I know, I know, Antonio. I could not believe it either. He's dead, Antonio. He died last night."

"How did this happen? How could he die? I just talked to him a few days ago."

I could barely hold the phone in my hand; I was shaking so badly.

Maria was sobbing so heavily she could barely speak. "He shot himself," she said. As she said that, I could hear the sound of Mrs. H and others weeping heavily in the background on the phone.

"No, that has to be a mistake," I said. "It had to have been an accident. Was he cleaning one of his guns and it went off?" I asked. I knew that this was not the case. The way Maria said, "He shot himself," followed by the wailing of his wife and mother in the background, suggested this was not an accident, but I did not want to believe he was gone, and that he had intentionally done this to himself . . . to us.

"It wasn't a mistake," Maria sobbed. "He drove to the place where he and his dad used to go duck hunting. He texted his wife and told her what he was going to do and then he shot himself. He's gone, Antonio; I'm so sorry. You are the first of his friends that we called. I know you loved him like a brother."

Tears pooled in my eyes, and I found it difficult to speak. I was choking on my own tongue. "Oh my God, Maria. I'm so sorry. I'm so sorry." I began to weep heavily. "He's gone? He's actually gone?" I said. "How is Mom?" I asked (referencing Mrs. H).

"She's a mess," Maria said. "She's here at the house. We all are. We are all hurting."

A long pause ensued. I was weeping on one side of the call, and I could hear Mrs. H, Maria, her sister, Mark's wife, and others crying on the other side.

"Can you do me a favor?" Maria asked.

"Anything," I sobbed. "Tell me what you need."

"I need you to call Pablo and Bryan and tell them what happened. I can't do it, and they need to know. It hurts so much right now."

"OK. OK," I said, followed by a long pause. "OK. OK."

That's all I could muster up to say at that moment. We continued to weep on the phone until I said, "I will call them now and tell them. I can't believe this is happening. Thank you for calling me. Tell Mom I love her. Tell her I'm so sorry. Tell her my heart is broken."

"I will do that," she said. "Thank you. Call me back and we'll figure out what do from here."

We then hung up the phone. I gathered myself together and walked downstairs. My daughter was five years old and was playing downstairs in the living room. I asked my wife to come into the dining room and sit on the couch. I managed to tell her what happened without crying. I felt so numb and was still in disbelief. She gasped and said, "Oh my God, Antonio, I'm so sorry. I know you loved him so much." I broke down and then began to sob heavily. I could not stop crying. My face was flushed, and I felt like I had a fever. My head was hurting, and I felt like I was going to vomit.

"I have to call the guys and tell them what's going on. Maria needs me to tell them."

Reader, let's pause here for a moment. As you can see that morning I suddenly and unexpectedly found myself in a situation where things were fine, until suddenly they weren't. Hearing the news of losing my brother, Mark, to suicide gutted me. It literally broke me. The only way I can articulate what it felt like was as though someone reached into my body and grabbed my stomach and ripped it from inside me. I had lost people that I loved before, but this was different. It hurt in a different way, and it flipped my world upside down. I was forced from a place of stability and predictability in my life into a season of grief that immediately grabbed ahold of me, and I was unprepared for the emotions that would follow. I would ask you to consider a moment in your life that upon hearing painful news things suddenly were "not fine." Reflect on the source of that grief and the physical and emotional feelings that accompanied it. Now I'm going to ask you to take a deep breath and close your eyes and whisper, "My yoke is easy, and my burden is light." Stay with those feelings for a moment and continue to repeat, "My yoke is easy, and my burden is light," and return to the conversation.

In 1969, Dr. Elisabeth Kübler-Ross published a book titled *On Death and Dying*. Her work is considered foundational to our understanding of grief in the field of psychology. Dr. Kübler-Ross conducted years of research interviewing patients who were terminally ill or were in the final stages of life receiving palliative care. She also interviewed families who were grieving the loss of a loved one. In her research, Dr. Kübler-Ross discovered that there were a few universal responses to grief that we all experience. No matter how young or old, rich or poor, powerful or weak, humans tended to react to loss similarly. She identified these reactions as the five stages of grief. The stages are denial, anger, bargaining, depression, and acceptance. While the stages are universal, the process of experiencing them is not. We may start at different stages and move to the next stage or skip a stage entirely. It is also possible to move through one stage of grief and then return to it weeks or months later. There is no clear timeline for how long we stay in each of these stages and there is not one concrete thing we can do to move us from one stage to the next. We learned from Dr. Kübler-Ross's work that grief is complex, highly individualized to each person, and a normal part of life. No one is immune from the stages, and we will all find ourselves experiencing them at some point, usually multiple times in our lives.[1]

I share this with you because the first stage of grief I encountered when I heard the news of Mark's passing was denial. You can see that my reaction to the news of his death was complete disbelief. I wanted to believe that it was someone other than my friend who had passed, or that the phone call was a joke. I wanted to believe his passing was an accident and not a suicide. I could not process the words I was hearing as Maria spoke to me over the phone. After years of processing my grief in the presence of spiritual mentors and through contemplative prayer, I learned that when I receive difficult news about losing someone or something in my life, my first reaction is often denial. I had to work through that denial to confront the reality that was placed in front of me, and that was difficult for me to do. Sometimes, when we grieve, we return to denial. Even after the funeral is over and a loved one has been buried, their surviving spouse still wakes

1. Kübler-Ross, *On Death and Dying*, ch. 11.

up in the middle of the night reaching for their partner in bed. Sometimes they come home to an empty house, looking for their spouse or child who passed away weeks ago. I remember listening on my cell phone to the last voicemail that Mark left me. I called his number on occasion after he had passed, still hoping he would answer, wishing his passing was just a horrible nightmare. I was stuck in the denial stage of grief. Now let's return to the story to learn more about how others might react when grief first grabs ahold of them.

My wife sat with me on the couch as I called my two other friends who are also like brothers to me and Mark. I called Pablo first. His reaction to the news was very different to mine. When I told Pablo that Mark had passed, his first reaction was anger. Pablo yelled, "What do you mean he's dead? Why would he do that? He has a wife and kids for God's sake!" When I tried to comfort Pablo by telling him that I too was hurting from hearing the news he said, "I'm not sad, I'm pissed. I want to go to the coroner's office right now and slap his corpse! *How could he leave us like that?* How could he do that to us, and his family, and mom?" He then began to weep heavily. I let him cry over the phone without saying a word. Pablo's reaction may sound cold and harsh, but that was the first stage of grief that hit him. It came from a deep place of pain that I knew was real, because I had never heard Pablo cry in my entire twenty years of knowing him. Not once.

The second phone call I made was to my other brother, Bryan. Bryan too reacted differently than me and Pablo. Bryan's reaction was a blend of bargaining and depression. When he heard the news that Mark passed, he immediately began to weep. "Oh my God. I just talked to him a couple of weeks ago. He was fine. This is so awful. I should have been there for him. If I had been there for him, maybe I could have changed his mind." Bryan immediately felt sadness and guilt over the loss of his friend. He felt as though he did not do enough for our brother who was hurting.

I told Bryan gently over the phone, "You know how much he struggled, Bryan. You know that once Mark made up his mind to do something, no one could talk him out of it."

"I know. You're right," be sobbed. "I just wish he would have told me how he was feeling. I would have done anything for him."

After the funeral, my brothers and I stayed in touch, but the interesting thing was that we didn't talk about Mark very much. When we saw each other over pizza, or spoke on the phone, we talked about how our lives were going, but rarely ever mentioned Mark. That may sound strange to some. Maybe even a little cold. It's not that we weren't hurting. We missed him painfully every day. I think that it was too raw and too soon for us to process our feelings with one another verbally, but we knew that we needed to be near one another in our time of grief. After Mark died, we did not have to work to see one another after his death. All the excuses we told each other about why we would push another poker night or pizza dinner to another date had disappeared. We actively sought each other out to spend time together, but we could not bring ourselves to talk about the empty chair at the table.

My grief continued to build for months after Mark's death. Sometimes I awoke in the middle of the night in tears, sweating heavily. I had nightmares of the day Maria told me, "Mark is dead," over and over. I could not eat, and I lost the motivation to exercise or socialize with my family or broader friend group. In the middle of the day, without any trigger or clear reason, I would be consumed by the overwhelming weight of sadness in my heart and weep for no reason. I could not prevent it from happening, and at times, the weeping would last for minutes on end. Sometimes I would need to get up from my chair and close the door to my office at work because I could feel a weeping spell coming on. I would sit in my office in tears, unable to work. I remember standing in the meat section of a supermarket where Mark and I used to go and buy the chickens we would roast in his backyard, and without warning, my eyes filled with tears. I left the store without buying anything and just sat in my car and wept.

I tried to manage my grief the best I could. I tried to consume myself with work and start new projects to distract me from my emotions. I went to church, but I felt so numb during the Mass that I could not hear the homily the priest was delivering. I wanted to tell my wife how I was feeling, but I did not want her to worry about me. At times I ate junk food to make me feel better temporarily or drank to try and numb the pain I was feeling. Nothing helped. In fact, my symptoms started to get too heavy for me to bear. The hurting was too much.

Before transitioning into a career in higher education, I worked in the field of child welfare. I was good at my job and had been promoted to a director position within my agency. The children and families we served had experienced great trauma in their lives, and many of the youth we served were part of the foster care or probation systems. They had been rejected by their biological families just like Mark had, and they too were managing their grief in unhealthy ways. We helped connect them with mental health services, educational support, and other resources as they struggled to maintain some sense of a normal life in the midst of their grief.

One day, a supervisor I worked with came to alert me that a child that was receiving services from our agency passed away from suicide. He was adopted by a loving family and struggled with substance abuse and depression his entire short life. He was fifteen when he hung himself in his closet. The note he left behind said he wished he knew his biological parents and that he could never understand why they hated him. It broke me. I could not keep Mark from ending his life and now I had experienced the death of another youth who had only known rejection, sorrow, and isolation. I was already unwell, and I did not know what to do. About six months after learning the news of the youth who passed in foster care, I left my job in child welfare. I pursued a job, still working with children since that was all I had done since graduating from college, but I had hoped the children I was working with may come with less trauma, allowing me time to work on my grief. The job ended up serving children with similar backgrounds and I again found myself in the same struggles I was experiencing in my previous work.

Finally, I reached my breaking point. William Hannan once said, "Sometimes all you can do is lie in bed and hope to fall asleep before you fall apart."[2] That is how I felt this particular morning when I called out sick because my grief had taken complete hold of me. I was wrapped in the throes of a debilitating depression, and something did not feel quite right within myself. I was hurting, and it was scary to me how hopeless I was feeling. I laid in bed for the majority of the morning, slipping in and out of sleep, only getting out of bed to use the restroom. I felt I could no longer carry the responsibilities of a husband and father, and that scared me. As I lay in bed, looking up at the ceiling, I said, "God, I don't know if I want to be here anymore. If I'm going to live every day feeling like this, then I don't want to be here anymore."

Suddenly, a quiet voice entered my thoughts. "Phil," it said. I thought it was odd, because I did not immediately recognize the name. "Phil," it said again. Then I realized: my favorite professor from my master's and doctoral program was Phil, but I called him Dr. M.

It had been three years since I had finished school, but on occasion, I would email Dr. M, just to say hello and tell him how I was doing. Dr. M was a brilliant and kind man. He taught several of the classes I took in my

2. Hannan, as cited in Cohen, "Grief Quotes."

graduate studies and had taken me under his wing. He encouraged me to apply for the doctoral program, even though I did not believe I was capable of the academic rigor, and he was boundlessly supportive of my education. He was tall, over six feet, and was lanky and walked on his tiptoes through the halls of the school. He always wore clothes that were ill fitting, wrinkled and in disarray, and I only saw him wear one pair of shoes the entire time I knew him. He had short white hair that wrapped around the sides of his head, and the top of his head was shiny and bald. He would speak in a low, gentle tone, and when he lectured, or we spoke in his office, he would rest one hand, balled in a gentle fist beneath his chin. The other arm crossed his chest as if he was holding himself. He would then close his eyes and say the most brilliant thought that the class or I had ever heard. Then he would slowly open his eyes and return to the conversation.

Dr. M also was a slow grader. It took weeks for us to receive our papers and grades once we had submitted them. But even though this was the case, we were always grateful to receive our feedback from him. During my studies, Dr. M would assign work that prompted the class to reflect on our personal backgrounds and struggles. Part of his job was to prepare us to enter the counseling field, and to help others understand their own trauma, we had to confront and understand our own. At the end of each paper, Dr. M would handwrite pages of feedback for every student. He would comment on our thoughts, offer resources for us to expand our learning, and leave long messages of encouragement personalized just for us. Every student looked forward to his assignments because though they were often challenging, we knew he would read every word we wrote and comment on them in a profound way.

He taught me the basic theories and techniques of counseling and taught other topics like ethics, proportionate reasoning, and leadership. He was also a man of God. He was a deep thinker with a Franciscan slant to his spirituality. Franciscans are a blend of contemplatives and philosophers. They are trained to be perpetually attune to the presence of God in all things and are deep and passionate thinkers. Franciscans also use the word "marrow" frequently to describe the source of an emotion. During our discussions, I had become accustomed to him asking me what I believe the marrow of a specific topic to be. He blended philosophy and theology seamlessly and sometimes after class, he would invite me to his office to talk about the topics I was studying. Occasionally, our discussion would turn to God. I was always amazed at the depth of his knowledge and understanding about God and spirituality. He would always end our meetings with a suggestion for an author or book that I should read. I would read them all and then revisit his office to discuss them with him. Sometimes he was so excited to suggest a book he would hop up from his chair and begin to frantically scan his bookshelves. "Where did I put that damn thing," he would mutter as he searched high and low amongst the hundreds of books chaotically stacked on shelves, his desk and on the floor. After sometimes minutes of searching, he'd hand me the book. The pages were bent and folded and highlighted. Nearly illegible notes were written all over the margins. If you were to scan the bookshelves in my office today, you would find the same thing happening with my books too. Only I stack them neatly.

I can't quite explain it, but after hearing the voice in my head whisper, "Phil," I suddenly felt compelled to reach out to him. I got out of bed and walked to my computer to email him. In my email, I shared that I was struggling immensely and told him about Mark's passing. I told him I was having difficulty getting out of bed in the morning, and I was hoping to talk to him as soon as possible. Within an hour, Dr. M, had responded. The email was short and simple. "Antonio, my heart is breaking for you. Let's talk." It was followed by a date and time to meet at his office.

I met with Dr. M on the date and time he provided me. As I sat in his office, I told him about all the pain I felt, and the ways I had attempted to cope with my feelings. But I did not tell him how it came to be that I emailed him. He listened intently, without saying a word. He often used long pauses during conversations for emotions to fill the spaces between thoughts. Then he said, "I'm so glad that you decided to talk to me about your feelings. May I ask how you came to think of reaching out to me during this difficult time?"

I immediately began to sob. I told him the feelings I was having the morning that grief had confined me to my bed. I told him of the feelings of hopelessness that were scaring me. I told him that I asked God if it was worth being here anymore, because the grief was so heavy. Another long pause ensued and as the tears ran down my face, Dr. M quietly closed his eyes, rested his chin upon his hand in that same familiar stance I had seen for so many years, and gently said, "Antonio, it sounds like you've been running from your grief for a long time, and it's finally caught up with you. You are not OK. You keep returning to and getting stuck in the denial stage."

I sobbed, "I don't know what else to do. It hurts too much. I can't keep carrying this weight anymore."

Then Dr. M asked, "Did you talk to God about any of those feelings before that morning in bed?"

"No," I said. "I've been so angry with him. Sometimes I wonder if he exists. How could he leave me in this pain?"

I'll never forget the words he said to me after that. Dr. M responded, "You can't be angry with something you don't believe exists. In your heart, you know God exists because you are upset with him. He has never left you, Antonio. He's been present with you in all of this. But did you notice that you didn't hear him until you spoke to him that morning in bed? And what did God do? He answered you immediately. He's been present with you in all of it. From a spiritual sense you've tried to carry this weight without talking to God. Your weight was so heavy, you could not hear him speaking to you the entire time. You've been searching for the yoke to help carry the weight."

Reader, if you are unfamiliar with the word, a yoke is a tool used by farmers that looks like a giant wooden frame that stretches across the backs of two beasts of burden. It connects two animals like horses or bison together to bear the massive weight of the plow that they pull behind them. Without the yoke, one beast could not plow the field alone. The weight was too heavy, and the work would eventually consume the beast with exhaustion. But with the yoke, two beasts could share the load, and the burden of the plow was made lighter. Together, they could carry the heavy weight of the work ahead.

I began to sob more heavily. I felt so meek and vulnerable, but Dr. M was right. Up until that moment, I had done everything I could to deny or avoid my grief without talking to God. I tried to carry it all on my own, and it was eating me alive. Another long pause ensued. Dr. M let me sit with my grief and weep in his office. I wept for a few minutes, and occasionally, I would look up to see tears rolling down Dr. M's face as he looked at me with a calm, peaceful gaze.

"Antonio," he said gently. "I'd like you to do something for me."

"OK," I said. "What should I do?"

"I want you to repeat after me. 'I sought the Lord, and he heard, and he answered.'"

"'I sought the Lord, and he heard, and he answered,'" I repeated through my sobs.

"'I sought the Lord, and he heard, and he answered,'" he said again.

"'I sought the Lord, and he heard, and he answered,'" I repeated.

"'My yoke is easy, and my burden is light,'" he said.

"'My yoke is easy, and my burden is light,'" I repeated.

"'My yoke is easy, and my burden is light,'" he said.

"'My yoke is easy, and my burden is light,'" I repeated.

"God is here with us right now, Antonio. He's present with us in this office. He was with you on the drive over. He was with you when you heard the news that Mark passed. He's with you right now. Sit with him and give your grief to him. Give that weight to him. His yoke is easy, and his burden is light."

"'His yoke is easy, and his burden is light,'" I repeated.

As I sat with Dr. M, repeating the verses he was sharing, I realized he was quoting Scripture. Psalm 34:4 says, "I sought the Lord, and he answered me; he delivered me from all my fears" (NIV). In Matt 11:30 Jesus says, "My yoke is easy, and my burden is light." After a few moments the pain I was feeling gradually subsided. My sobs slowly faded away, and I felt so tired that I could sleep for days. Dr. M and I sat in God's presence, in silence, while a wave of peace flooded over me that I had not felt since before Mark had passed.

"Thank you, Dr. M. I've never felt that kind of peace before," I said.

"You can do this anytime the hurting becomes too much, Antonio," Dr. M gently said.

"Is this meditation?" I asked.

"It's called centering prayer, Antonio. And it's helped me through several very difficult moments in my life. Now I practice centering prayer every day. And it helps me remain conscious of God's presence in every moment of my day."

At that moment, I pictured Mr. H standing next to me, smiling. I was reminded of his promise that he would teach me how to center when he was alive.

Centering prayer is an ancient form of contemplative prayer attributed to the work of Brother Lawrence in the seventeenth century. Brother Lawrence was a layperson who served in a Carmelite monastery in France. His teachings were later published in a book called *The Practice of the Presence of God*. I highly recommend you take the time to read this important work. Brother Lawrence believed there was no start or end time to prayer, rather every moment of every day was an opportunity to worship and adore God in our daily actions. There was no difference in adoring Christ between cooking or washing dishes or sitting in front of the Blessed Sacrament in church.[3] Every action we complete in our day is intended to glorify God in the process. Practicing centering prayer and maintaining the awareness of the perpetual presence of God in all things is a humbling process. It reminds me of the famous speech Dr. Martin Luther King Jr. delivered in 1967 when he said:

> If a man is called to be a street sweeper, he should sweep streets even as Michelangelo painted, or Beethoven composed music or Shakespeare wrote poetry. He should sweep streets so well that all the hosts in heaven and earth with pause to say, "Here lived a great street sweeper who did his job well."[4]

Engaging in what Brother Lawrence called "the perpetual practice of the presence of God"[5] is a spiritual discipline that invites the person into a loving conversation with God throughout the entire day, no matter how small or insignificant our actions may seem. Brother Lawrence often spoke to God continuously throughout the day and, in moments of silence, sat in the presence of God and focused on a Scripture verse or word to guide his adoration. Brother Lawrence taught that in centering prayer, you were not talking to Jesus. You were encountering him. From that moment forward, I began to practice centering prayer once a day, sometimes even two or three times, if needed.

Dr. M and I continued to meet for discussions long after that first vulnerable evening in his office. It was difficult at times, but he helped me identify the stages of grief I was experiencing and also helped me name the emotions I was feeling. Then we would center in his office at the end of each meeting, reciting the verse: "My yoke is easy, my burden is light." For me, it took about a year before I could confidently say that the hurting would no longer consume me. I was no longer bound by my grief. I was walking with it. That did not mean that I had stopped missing Mark. I thought of him almost every day. But my grief didn't consume me in the way it had before, and I discovered I could even experience moments of happiness in the midst of grieving his loss. I had learned to carry, as Fr. Rohr had stated, a "bright sadness, sober happiness or luminous darkness." I was living "the simultaneous existence of deep suffering and intense joy."[6]

3. Lawrence, *Practice of the Presence of God*, 15.
4. King, *I Have a Dream*, 34.
5. Lawrence, *Practice of the Presence of God*, 11–12.
6. Rohr, *Falling Upward*, 75.

From that moment on, centering prayer and other contemplative forms of prayer were a part of my daily routine. When I awoke in the morning, before an important meeting at work, on my lunch break, or during my drive home, and right before I slipped into a deep sleep for the night, I centered. One of my favorite contemplative practices I use is reciting the Jesus Prayer. The Jesus Prayer is an ancient "arrow prayer" recited by monks who wandered in the Egyptian desert around the fourth or fifth century. Monks had fled the epicenters of most major metropolises to find God. At that time, the church, and Christianity as a religion, was becoming more formalized. As laws and mandates were imposed by the church, some of them unjust and oppressive, monks retreated to the desert seeking to strengthen their relationship with Christ. They were worried that the rules of religion would replace spirituality and they sought to reconnect with their love for Jesus. They would recite the prayer, sometimes placing an emphasis on one specific word, like: "*Lord*, Jesus Christ, son of God, have mercy on me, a sinner." Or "Lord, Jesus Christ, son of *God*, have mercy on me, a sinner." Or "Lord, Jesus Christ, son of God, have *mercy* on me, a sinner." Or "Lord, Jesus Christ, son of God, have mercy on me, a *sinner*."

If you think about it, the Jesus Prayer evolved from grief. Monks fled to the desert, grieving the rules of religion that distracted them from the gospel's message. They sought to be biblically rooted, but they also did not want to forget that Jesus called us to practice our faith. "Christlikeness," as we sometimes say, was becoming second to knowledge of Scripture. They sought a balance of knowing God's word and living it. The Jesus Prayer was a reminder of Jesus's perpetual presence, and also a call to humble ourselves before him and seek his mercy. Every night, as I lie in bed, and just as sleep is starting to overpower me, I slip away and whisper, "Lord, Jesus Christ, son of God, have mercy on me, a sinner." They are the last words to leave my mouth every night.

I share this with you because contemplative prayer gave me a starting point for what are now daily conversations with God. I can't go a day without talking to him. I pause during the busy rush of meetings and classes to recite the Jesus Prayer, or center on a Scripture verse, or engage in the Lectio Divina or Daily Examen (I will discuss those in subsequent chapters). It has become a routine that has led me to deep reflection of events that have transpired in my life, and where God has been present in all of them. Each morning, when I first wake up, I recite the arrow prayer that Mother Teresa of Calcutta used to say. Just three simple words. "Good morning,

Jesus." That's it. When my eyes open, I say, "Good morning, Jesus," and then proceed to go for a walk and then center before getting ready for work.

If you are in the midst of your own grief, and are feeling as though the hurting is too much, I would ask you to reflect upon the last time you talked to God. Was that recently or has it been some time since you sat with him in a quiet place and openly shared what you are going through? Have you sought the only yoke that can truly carry your burdens with you? What are you replacing his yoke with? Food, work, alcohol, tobacco, cannabis, pornography, sleep, denial, or anger? All of these things have the appearance of a yoke, but they don't carry the weight. They only distract you from it. You continue to carry the weight by yourself until, like me, it catches up with you. Eventually, these false yokes crumble away and the grief you are feeling is finally felt again, only it is heavier each time you are confronted with it.

I would humbly recommend that you talk to a counselor, pastor, priest, or close mentor about your feelings and talk to God. Sit with God and recite the Scriptures: "I sought the Lord, and he heard, and he answered." And, "My yoke is easy, and my burden is light." God is with you, asking to place your suffering upon his shoulders. He's trying to remind you that he's carried grief before. He knows what it's like to lose someone that he loves dearly and he's here with you now to carry that burden with you. Surrender to Jesus's invitation to carry your burdens and you will find, as I did, that your life will never be the same. There is a path through the stages of grief, and Jesus has carved that path out for us. On the other side, we find joy, and like the tenth leper who was healed and returned to him, we fall at his feet to give him thanks for walking with us in our grief. The lesson I learned from Dr. M that day in his office and after ten years of practicing contemplative prayer is that when grief strikes suddenly and deeply, we enter into a spiritual process of seeking the yoke. It is the first step to our spiritual grief work. Find the yoke, and you find Jesus. Find Jesus and you find strength. Find strength and you find a path through the stages of grief. Find a path through the stages, and you find a joy that overpowers any feeling grief can offer. Don't be afraid to search for the yoke. It's worth the risk.

3

Why Do You Doubt?

"Grief is like the ocean; It [*sic*] comes in waves; ebbing and flowing. Sometimes the water is calm, and sometimes it is overwhelming. All we can do is learn to swim."

—Vicki Harrison

My father joined the Navy when he was eighteen years old during the conflict in Vietnam. He joined the Navy to escape the gang violence and lack of opportunities that plagued his community in Compton, California. Throughout my childhood, my father would occasionally share stories of his time in the military. He served as a radioman on a refueling and rearmament vessel called the USNS *Kawishiwi*. The ship's job was to replenish fuel and ammunition of US warships during the conflict. His ship was something like a floating gas station and ammo silo combined. The crew's mission was to sail into combat zones to quickly replenish warships who were actively engaged in combat. He described that on several occasions, small enemy boats would attempt to chase down their ship and shoot at it, in the hopes of igniting the fuel and ammo on board. The captain would have to take evasive maneuvers to outrun the enemy boats or risk being blown out of the water. While the enemy was certainly one threat that jeopardized the safety of the sailors aboard the ship, my father stated that another threat was equally terrifying. When their crew wasn't fighting the enemy, it was surviving the massive storms at sea.

He described that during the intense storms, the waves were so big, he thought they would consume the entire ship. His job as a radioman required him to be on the bridge of the ship so he had a clear view of the horizon in front of him. During the storms, he said that the waves would lift the entire bow of the ship out of the water. During these terrifying moments, all he could see was the sky and storm clouds above him. Then as the ship came crashing down onto the wave, the sky disappeared and was replaced by the ocean below. He could no longer see the sky or the clouds, only the ocean that appeared to be consuming the ship below and beside him. He said it looked as though the entire ship was plunging straight into the ocean. When he told me this story, he could still hear the groans and creaking of the ship's massive steel hull buckling under its own weight. He also knew when the storms were especially dangerous because on the bridge, he was responsible for messaging the captain's communications to nearby ships. At times he could detect the slight panic and concern in the captain's voice. It was in those moments that he knew how close the ship was to being consumed by the massive waves.

As an eighteen-year-old man who had never left his block in Compton, he was terrified. He said there were moments he was convinced that he was going to die there in the open ocean due to the storm's violent waves. There's a saying in the military that "there are no atheists in fox holes." This was certainly true during those moments at sea. During the storms, men who stated they did not practice any religion or believe in God suddenly started praying to anything and everything to help them survive the storm. Fear brought grown men to their knees and prompted them to pray for their own survival. Eventually, the storm would pass, and my dad described how the entire mood of the crew would change. There was a peace present that lasted for days, but eventually, another storm would return. Living and working on the ship required the sailors to live in seasons of calm and stormy seas. And these seasons could change with little to no warning.

In the previous chapter I shared a personal account of when grief took ahold of me unexpectedly, and I found myself stuck in the denial stage of grief. I also shared the stages of grief and my introduction to contemplative prayer as a means of engaging in a dialogue with God that helped me move through the stages of my grief. In the early stages of walking with my grief, a mentor helped me identify the source of my grief, the stages I passed through, and helped me to name the feelings associated with them. This is helpful to people struggling with grief because it gives us a starting point for our grief work. But as we begin the process of walking with grief, it is also helpful to know that grief presents itself with a multitude of symptoms. These symptoms are powerful and disruptive to our well-being. From a psychological perspective, we want to listen to and identify these symptoms since they are our body's and mind's way of signaling to us that something is wrong. The symptoms are a by-product of our feelings and call for us to take time to address the source of our discomfort. Just like when a physical diagnosis of cancer presents symptoms, we don't want to only treat the symptoms and leave the source of our illness unaddressed. If we were to only treat the symptoms without treating the cancer, our life would be in jeopardy. Grief work is similar in this way. We want to be aware of the symptoms we are experiencing and recognize the underlying condition that is causing them. This is easier said than done.

The field of psychology teaches us that when we experience emotional distress, like grief, emotional and physiological symptoms are often present. These symptoms can occur singularly or simultaneously and can come and go as we begin our journey of grief work. Some of the symptoms of grief are:

1. Appetite (increased/decreased)
2. Anxiety
3. Depression
4. Irritability
5. Self-harm, or self-injurious behaviors
6. Lack of motivation
7. Apathy
8. Decreased libido
9. Increased alcohol consumption
10. Using substances to cope with feelings of distress
11. Lack of trust in others
12. Inability to enjoy activities you once loved
13. Isolation
14. Guilt/shame
15. Sarcasm

16. Separation anxiety
17. Confusion (sudden onset caused by small changes)
18. Obsessive dwelling on the past
19. Apprehension about the future
20. Decrease in the quantity or quality of sleep
21. Increased desire to sleep to avoid feelings of distress

This is not an exhaustive list, and as you may notice, these symptoms are not isolated to grief alone. Other physiological and emotional conditions can cause them. But if you have experienced a significant loss in your life, and find that you are unwell emotionally or physically, these may be signs that your grief needs to be addressed. So, we start with identifying the source(s) of our grief. We move on to naming the emotions that accompany our grief. We search for the yoke or the presence of God in the midst of our grief and engage in frequent dialogue with him and our support systems, and then we begin to identify the symptoms of grief that are manifesting in our lives. It all sounds so simple, right? Please give yourself some grace. For me, this process took about a year. A year of constant conversations with my mentor, daily prayer and contemplation, and at times, medication to assist me in my grief work. It was a year of inching over the bridge of my grief to meet Christ on the other side, and to realize that with every step, my grief weakened and the symptoms slowly subsided. If you are currently walking with your grief and find yourself stepping backwards at times instead of forward, again, give yourself grace. The process is not linear, and every person's journey is different. I would recommend for you to continue to lean into your conversations with God who is forever present and continue to communicate with your network at each step in the journey. It may also help to remind yourself that in a sense, grief doesn't end. Try not to expect yourself to one day be "over" or "past" your grief; rather, remind yourself that grief evolves. It will evolve into something that is eventually manageable and can even teach us to find joy in the small moments in life which will certainly follow.

The symptoms of grief are like a storm at sea. They can come on suddenly and without warning and when they do, it can feel like we will be consumed by them entirely. The tricky thing about grief is, the more you try to fight it, the more it hurts. Grief is not something intended to be eradicated or cured. If we are to address the symptoms we are experiencing, then, we have to submit to our grief and learn to ride out the storm. How grief takes hold of us, and the extent to which it consumes us, has a lot to do with how we posture ourselves towards grief when it first presents itself. Just as you cannot control the storm, neither can you control your grief. At some point, the sailors on my father's ship had to accept that the storm will come, and it will be heavy, but it will also pass.

One day, during one of the heavier conversations I had with my mentor when discussing my grief, I experienced a backtracking of sorts. I had been doing well with processing my grief around Mark's passing for about a month, and I seemed to be headed in the right direction. It was about a year since he had passed, and I had been working hard on addressing the source of my grief which was providing me with moments of relief from the symptoms I was experiencing. As I had mentioned earlier, Mark passed on February 15, 2015. As the first anniversary of Mark's death approached, I was looking forward to celebrating Valentine's Day with my wife. I was focused on where we would celebrate and the gift I was going to give her. Suddenly, about a week prior to Valentine's Day, I remembered the anniversary of Mark's passing and it consumed me. I found my motivation to celebrate Valentine's Day with my wife decreasing with every passing moment, and suddenly my feelings of joyful anticipation to celebrate an evening with my wife suddenly turned to thoughts of sadness. During my morning centering prayer, I spoke to God about how I was feeling. I told him that I was torn between celebrating with my wife and grieving the loss of my friend. To be honest, I was struggling and realized I was headed back into a period of denial, where I thought I could celebrate with my wife and pretend as though I wasn't still missing my friend. I was telling myself I could handle it. After all, I had been doing well emotionally for about a month. I arrogantly thought I could remove the yoke and carry my grief on my own. I'd like to share an experience I had when engaging in a moment of contemplative prayer that helped bring me back to the marrow of my walk with grief.

In addition to centering prayer, another form of contemplative prayer I practice is called the Lectio Divina. The term is Latin and, translated, means "the divine word." It is an ancient practice with roots in Jewish practices of scriptural reflection that was adopted by monasteries around the sixth century. By that time, St. Benedict was promoting the practices widely within monasteries, and this form of contemplative prayer eventually evolved into a four-step process that was adopted by the Second Vatican Council in the twentieth century. While the method of engaging in the Lectio Divina has evolved over the centuries, the focus remains constant, which is to enter into a conversation with God that deepens our contemplation of his presence in our lives and thus transforms our interaction with the world.

Practicing the Lectio Divina involves sitting in a quiet place, free of distractions. Focus is given to a specific piece of Scripture where one reads, reflects, responds, and rests in the word of God. The individual surrenders to the presence of the Holy Spirit who places us in the context of the word. These steps therefore are not always experienced as linear or progressive, rather they can appear more like "moments" rather than a process. In the presence of the Holy Spirit, and while progressing through these four stages, we experience the Scripture as active participants. We are no longer only reading the Scripture to analyze and memorize it; rather, we become active participants in the story. We are present with the characters in the Scripture and are participants in the events taking place. For this reason, the Lectio Divina is a powerful tool that summons the spontaneity and wisdom of the Holy Spirit and is a very dynamic and emotional experience.

During our session, I told my mentor that I was feeling trapped by the symptoms that suddenly hit without warning. I told him I was feeling guilty for my experiencing those symptoms since they were inhibiting me from enjoying the anticipation of celebrating Valentine's Day with my wife. He listened intently and said, "Antonio, I think you've made tremendous progress in walking with your grief. The storm has returned and it's making it difficult for you to stay fixed on the horizon. The horizon is God. The horizon is life. I want you to keep your eyes on Jesus. He's telling you that it doesn't have to be joy or sadness. It can be both. But remember, you need to allow him to carry that grief with you. Have you considered that the grief you are feeling can actually help you appreciate the moments with your wife more deeply?" He was right. I was looking at the situation through a lens of either/or. I was either going to be happy or sad. But Jesus teaches us that grief work is not about the dualistic mentality of either/or. It's both/and. I was not allowing myself to realize that I could, in fact, feel both emotions at the same time. I could both miss my friend and joyfully anticipate the time of celebration with my wife. Grief is both progression and regression. Grief is both joy and sorrow. Grief is tied up in both the present and the past. It's the "luminous darkness" and the "sober happiness" that Rohr described. He then encouraged me to go home and engage in the Lectio Divina, focused on the Scripture from Matt 14:22–33 when Peter walks on water.

Reader, I am going to share that Scripture with you now and ask you to engage in the Lectio Divina with me. I am going to ask you to enter into the same contemplative space that I did that evening, and following our exercise, I will share what God revealed to me during that moment of deep contemplation. I am going to ask that you set time aside for the following activity, about twenty to thirty minutes. Keep your Bible and this book close and allow yourself to move through this exercise without any distractions. Let's begin.

I'm going to ask you to read the Scripture from Mark 14:22–33 first so that you understand the story that unfolds, and the characters involved. In Matt 14:22–33 (NABRE) it says:

> Then he made the disciples get into the boat and precede him to the other side, while he dismissed the crowds. After doing so, he went up on the mountain by himself to pray. When it was evening he was there alone. Meanwhile the boat, already a few miles offshore, was being tossed about by the waves, for the wind was against it. During the fourth watch of the night, he came toward them, walking on the sea. When the disciples saw him walking on the sea they were terrified. "It is a ghost," they said, and they cried out in fear. At once [Jesus] spoke to them, "Take courage, it is I; do not be afraid." Peter said to him in reply, "Lord, if it is you, command me to come to you on the water." He said, "Come." Peter got out of the boat and began to walk on the water toward Jesus. But when he saw how [strong] the wind was he became frightened; and, beginning to sink, he cried out, "Lord, save me!" Immediately Jesus stretched out his hand and caught him, and said to him, "O you of little faith, why did you doubt?" After they got into the boat, the wind died down. Those who were in the boat did him homage, saying, "Truly, you are the Son of God."

Now that you've read the story, I'd like to provide a little context for the passage so it will help with the next stage of the process. Let's unpack the story a little bit more. Prior to this Scripture, Jesus and the disciples had just experienced a few traumatic events. In fact, it is not farfetched to say that Jesus and the disciples were experiencing their own grief long before the storm rocked their boat. You see, chapter 14 in Matthew starts with King Herod expressing his opinion of Jesus. Herod, the reigning king and symbol of power and wealth over all the land, officially declares that he believes that Jesus is a threat. Herod essentially declares Jesus an enemy of the state. He has put a bull's-eye over Jesus's back and has stated that he is disrupting the natural order and strategic plan of the empire. He's a rebel that needs to be treated as an enemy of the state. So, Jesus and his disciples are aware that they are officially targets of the government and all its power. They are no longer a small band of hopefuls, quietly subverting the empire. They are now a full-blown threat to its laws, economy, and presence. That alone can evoke stress and worry within the disciples.

If that wasn't enough, Herod demonstrates his power to his subjects by ordering the incarceration and execution of John the Baptist. Herod is angry with John the Baptist for challenging his power and rousing the people. In a moment of anger and lust for the daughter of Herodias, he orders for John the Baptist to be beheaded. John, who was already incarcerated for challenging the empire, is now brutally executed. The Scripture says the disciples came and took away the corpse of John that Baptist and then told Jesus what happened. John the Baptist was Jesus's cousin. They knew each other well and John even baptized Jesus, officially launching the beginning of his ministry. King Herod essentially made a clear statement to Jesus, the disciples, and all subjects in the kingdom: "Look what I do to people who challenge my power."

Imagine the fear that entered the hearts of the disciples upon being labeled as enemies of the state, and now seeing the brutal murder of someone labeled as such by the king. Also, imagine the pain Jesus was going through, knowing his cousin was unjustly incarcerated and savagely murdered for preaching of the Messiah. The disciples and Jesus were consumed by grief from the murder of their friend and were worried that they too would be next. They identified the source of their grief, and were each going through the stages of grief, and now were experiencing the symptoms of grief that were consuming them. The disciples weren't OK.

Scripture tells us after the death of John the Baptist that Jesus went off alone in a boat to a deserted place. I can only imagine what Jesus was thinking and speaking to his Father on that boat. Jesus was hurting. He needed to step away from his ministry for a moment to connect with the yoke that sustained him. He confided in his Father and probably shared the feelings that were weighing on him, and the symptoms of grief he was experiencing. He sat on the water, talking to his Father. His mentor. His yoke. He struggled with the horrors and injustices he had witnessed. Jesus then, in a sense, was not OK.

So, the disciples were not OK. Jesus was not OK. But the problems that plagued the world continued. Scripture tells us then when people learned the location of Jesus, they followed him along the shoreline. Soon just a few people turned into a crowd of five thousand. Thousands of people were pursuing Jesus as he sat in solitude because they too were not OK. The crowd was composed of the sick and the poor. The oppressed and the marginalized. The homeless and the meek. It says in Scripture that Jesus saw the crowds gathering and that "his heart was moved with pity for them" (Matt 22:14 NABRE). This is evidence of collective grief. Jesus and the community were hurting.

After all this trauma, and in the midst of intense grief, Jesus and the disciples return to their ministry. Jesus picks up with the work, healing the sick and preaching to the crowds. Imagine the pain that Jesus was feeling in his heart. He was grieving the loss of his cousin, anticipating the backlash that was to come from the empire, and was now addressing the dividedness and hate in the world by comforting the thousands of people who came to visit him.

The disciples needed to support Jesus in his ministry and continue spreading the word even after burying a dear friend. In spite of the heaviness of the events of the previous days, Jesus performs another miracle. He fed a crowd of five thousand sick and weary travelers with five loaves of bread and two fish. The disciples were astounded. They could barely stand under the physical exhaustion and grief they were feeling, let alone comprehend how Jesus managed to provide for the needs of another massive crowd. The past few days leading up to the storm on the sea were incredibly chaotic, filled with violence, death, and grief. Finally, at the end of the day, Jesus and the disciples, exhausted and grief-stricken, dismiss the crowds. Let's now continue with our activity. As you engage in the next steps of your contemplation, I'm going to ask the following of you:

1. Find a quite space free of distractions for at least the next thirty minutes.
2. Take a moment to create an awareness of your breathing and body posture.
3. Take slow, deep breaths and exhale slowly.
4. Relax the muscles in your arms, legs, and back.
5. Sit comfortably and draw into the presence of Jesus and continue to take slow, deep breaths.
6. Jesus is present with you in the room at this very moment.

7. He is sitting with you as you breathe slowly and deeply, sharing the space with you.
8. Let everything in your mind slip away. For the duration of this exercise, nothing else matters. Neither the past nor future is of concern. The only thing that matters is that you are here with Jesus in this moment.
9. Now I'm going to ask you to read this description of the events again, but this time, you are not a passive observer. You are on the boat with the disciples on the sea. You are a part of the story that is unfolding.

Continue to breath slowly and deeply and remain attuned to Jesus's presence as you continue to read. Picture yourself sitting on the large, wooden boat. It's evening and the orange sun is just beginning to dip below the horizon. The sky is darkening, giving way to night. A cool breeze brushes against your face and across your arms. You can feel the temperature dropping quickly with each passing moment. Take a moment to smell the sea. It's not quite as briny as the ocean. It smells more like a mixture of fresh air with a hint of algae, like a lake. Listen to the wooden hull creaking gently as the waves calmly lift the boat up and down and side to side. You can hear the waves gently crash against the hull. As you gaze around the boat you see the twelve disciples. They look exhausted. Some look close to tears. Some are sitting on the deck of the boat, their eyes gently closing as their heads bob up and down, attempting to fight the fatigue and sleep that is overwhelming them.

A few of the other disciples are standing on the boat, talking about the past few days. They are heartbroken. Peter seems to be struggling the most. His shoulders look heavy, and his posture looks as though he is emotionally defeated. He quietly wipes the thick tears running from his eyes as he gazes at the shoreline that is slipping out of view. It appears his grief grows with the distance they gain from the shore. The deeper the sea, the deeper his sadness. Some of the disciples are in awe of the miracles they just witnessed. Jesus was healing one sick person after another, and then, he fed a crowd of five thousand people! They struggled to find the words to describe what just happened. In the midst of so much brokenness and need, Jesus sent the crowd away with joyful tears in their eyes. They feasted in the midst of great sorrow. Some were laughing and telling each other how exciting it was to hear Jesus speak in person. The disciples were confused how so much hope and joy could bubble forth from the depths of severe exhaustion and grief. Some of the disciples are asking one another if they think Jesus is OK. He must be suffering emotionally from the death of his cousin. He's been going off on his own more frequently these past few days to talk to his Father. He's alone right now, as we speak, on a mountaintop praying. What will come of him in his grief, they wonder. What will come of us?

The boat gently rocks with the sea's pace, and the sunset gives way to the night sky. The stars shine brightly, reflecting against the water's smoothness. It's about 3 a.m. now and all of the disciples are asleep on the deck of the boat. You can hear the snores of the men and watch some of them shift and turn in their sleep. All except for one. Peter is still awake. He's sitting on the deck of the boat, his knees are raised to his chest with his arms wrapped around them, and his head is buried forward in his lap. He almost looks like he is sleeping, but the quiet sobs and shaking shoulders reveal to you he is in deep despair. You watch him weep alone on the deck when suddenly the breeze begins to stiffen.

The breeze turns into strong gusts of wind that begin to rock the boat harshly. The sea's glassy complexion begins to swell, and the waves quickly become choppy. Peter looks up; with tears in his eyes, he peers at the sky. So do you. The stars are gone. They've been consumed by thick black rain clouds. A heavy, cold rain begins to dump buckets of water into the boat. The disciples start to panic as the waves batter the hull. The bow is hurled upwards into the sky, only to come crashing down into the sea below you. You can only see moments of sky and water as the wind rips across the deck. The storm is unrelenting, and the disciples begin to scream, "We're going to die! The sea is going to consume us!" You struggle to keep your balance in the midst of the storm. Your heart races and your hands shake as you take note of your proximity to the side of the boat. You are terrified you will be tossed overboard into the stormy sea. Chaos and fear fill the boat. What are just a few moments of the unrelenting storm feels like days. Suddenly, someone cries out, "What is that?"

"Do you see that?" another disciple yells.

You can hardly hear their voices over the howling wind and raging sea.

"It's a ghost!" Peter yells. "It's walking on water!"

"Impossible!" another disciple yells. "It must be a ghost!"

You strain your eyes into the distance. You can barely make out the appearance of a soft glow through the wind, rain, and sea water that is being whipped up into the sky. As you squint into the distance, through the storm and the darkness, you see the silhouette of a man. He seems to be walking calmly on the waves. It looks like he is gliding across the top of the chaotic swells, steadily making his way to the boat. You wipe your eyes in disbelief, and squint again in the darkness. You can't believe what you are seeing. The fear intensifies on the boat. Some of the disciples call out to God. "Please save us, God! Don't let us die on the sea!"

You and the disciples struggle to stand as the figure approaches the boat. You grab on to one another in the chaos, staring in disbelief at how this man can walk calmly on the water, unfazed by the raging storm. As the figure approaches, Peter realizes that it is Jesus. "Jesus!" He yells. "Save us from the storm! We're going to die."

Immediately Jesus responds calmly, "It's me, Peter. Don't be afraid. It's OK. You're OK." Jesus is standing on the waves just a few feet out from the boat now.

No one can believe their eyes. Jesus is standing calmly, undisturbed by the storm. His face looks calm and confident. The boat is heaving under the violent waves, and the wind and the rain is threatening to shatter the boat to pieces. You are not quite sure how much more abuse the boat can take. Something has to give . . . soon.

Peter, weeping and terrified, appears confused by Jesus's presence. He is scared the storm will consume him. He glances at the waves in fear before fixing his eyes back on Jesus. Peter yells out to Jesus again. "Lord, if it's really you . . . tell me to come to you on the water!" Peter sounds as if he's daring and pleading with Jesus simultaneously. He still doesn't believe what he's seeing, but it's the only way he'll feel safe . . . to stand where Jesus is standing in the storm.

Without missing a beat, standing on the waves, Jesus stretches out his hand to Peter and says, "Come."

Peter staggers to the side of the boat. He shuffles quickly, taking tiny steps as the deck rises and falls below his feet. In fear, like a toddler calling out to his father, Peter yells, "Don't leave me Jesus! I'm coming! Please don't leave me, Lord! I'm so scared! I don't want to die!"

Jesus smiles. His eyes stay fixed on Peter. Jesus remains calm, patiently waiting for him to step out onto the sea. "It's OK, Peter. You're OK. Come to me."

The disciples on the boat cry out to Peter, "What are you doing? You'll die out there! Stay here with us!"

Peter shuffles with determination to the end of the boat and straddles the railing on the deck. One foot is hanging over the side of the boat and dips into the sea. The other slides back and forth on the soaked wooden deck. Peter lies face down on the railing, clinging to the boat.

"Rabbi! Please save me! I don't want to die. I won't make it!"

Jesus stays silent, reaching out calmly to Peter as he stands on the waves. Peter pushes his chest off the railing until he is sitting up straight. He slings both legs over the rail and steps out onto water. You and the disciples gasp at what you are witnessing. Peter is standing on top of the waves! The rain is pounding, and the winds are howling over the sea's crashing waves. The boat continues to bounce like a toy in the water, but Peter is standing on the waves, reaching out to Jesus. He begins to take baby steps towards Jesus. Peter is walking on water too!

You and the disciples cheer in disbelief. "He's doing it! He's walking to Jesus! Go Peter! Go!"

Jesus smiles at Peter and with an encouraging tone says, "It's OK. You're OK. Come to me, Peter. Come to me."

Peter smiles for a moment until an enormous wave crashes down over the top of the boat. You and the disciples scream in fear as the wave tosses all of you across the deck. The disciples slide back and forth on the deck, screaming in fear. Peter turns back to look at the boat. It looks like it's going to sink beneath the waves. He begins to panic at the thought of losing his friends.

Seeing Peter in distress, Jesus calls out to him, "Peter! Look at me. Look right into my eyes. I'm here, Peter. I'm right here. It's OK! You're OK! Come to me, Peter!"

"I can't, Lord!" Peter yells. "I'm scared! I can't take another step. I'm going to drown!"

"Look at me, Peter," Jesus replies. "I'm right here. I'm always with you. Trust me, Peter. Come to me."

"Go to him!" the disciples yell. "Go to Jesus, Peter! You're almost there!"

Peter breaks his gaze with Jesus. He starts to look at the waves that are blasting against the side of the boat. The rain is falling so hard it is stinging his face, and the wind is chilling his body to the bone. Suddenly, Peter begins to sink into the sea beneath him. His arms flail wildly in the water and within seconds, he is being tossed violently in the sea with the boat nearby.

Peter is fighting to keep the sea's water from entering his mouth and lungs. He's kicking as hard as he can to keep his head above the waves. One of his hands is shooting out from the waves as he gasps for air.

"Lord, save me!" he yells.

Without hesitation, as soon as Peter yells out to Jesus, a hand grabs his. It's Jesus!

Jesus, still standing on the waves, immediately grabs Peter's hand and begins lifting him up from the sea.

As he pulls Peter up from the water, he calmly looks into his eyes and gently smiles. In a deep, calm tone he whispers to him, "Oh Peter, your faith is so small sometimes. Why did you doubt?"

Peter is weeping as Jesus pulls him up out of the water and into the boat. You watch the disciples run to the railing to help pull Peter out of the water. He collapses, weeping heavily as he flops onto the soaking-wet deck. Peter is dripping wet and shivering from the brutal wind. He's spitting up water and coughing violently in between sobs.

Jesus climbs into the boat and drops to both knees besides Peter. He takes Peter in his arms and rocks him back and forth like the shepherd who finds the lost sheep and rubs his back to warm him up. In the gentlest tone of a mother talking to her weeping child, Jesus whispers, "It's OK, Peter. You're OK. Shhh . . . you're OK, my friend. I'm right here. Oh, Peter, why do you doubt?"

"I was so scared," Peter sobs. "I wanted to come to you, Lord, but the waves . . . they were too big. I'm so sorry, Jesus!"

Jesus continues to hug Peter on the deck of the boat and then turns his head to the storm clouds above him. He looks up at the storm and waves his hand across the sky. In an instant, the storm subsides. The winds vanish. The rain stops, and the sea returns to its smooth and glassy texture. The sky is as silent as the disciples who are spellbound by what they see. The only sounds that can be heard are the gentle waves and the creaky boat, are the sobs of Peter in Jesus arms.

"Shhh . . . it's OK, Peter. I'm right here. It's OK. You're OK, Peter," Jesus whispers.

At that moment, you and the disciples fall to your knees on the deck of the boat and prostrate yourselves before Jesus. "Truly you are the Son of God," you say. The disciples repeat, "This is the Son of God."

Reader, I'm going to ask you to pause for a moment and reflect upon the feelings that surfaced during this moment of contemplation. Reflect upon the events that occurred and remain present with the Lord. He's still present with you in the room. In the presence of Jesus, I'm going to ask you to reflect on the following questions:

1. What was the source of grief in this story?
2. What stages of grief were Jesus and his disciples experiencing?
3. What symptoms of grief were present in the story?
4. What feelings surfaced for you as an active participant in the Scripture?
5. What was Jesus's response during the story?
6. What do you want to say to Jesus this very moment, in his presence? Say that to him now, out loud.

Stay with those thoughts and feelings for a few moments. Rest in Jesus's presence, close your eyes, and take slow, deep breaths, in through the nose and out through the mouth. It may be helpful for you to open your Bible and read Matt 14:22–33 again, inserting yourself into the story. Then please come back to this book.

You have just completed a version of the Lectio Divina. During our contemplative session, you moved through the four steps of the Lectio Divina when you read the Scripture as an active participant in the story, reflected upon your reaction to the Scripture, responded to God's revelations in that moment, and rested in the presence of Jesus. This process can feel different every time you engage with the word of God, and you will find that even after reflecting upon the same verses multiple times, you may experience different emotions and connections to the Scripture. This is normal and can lead to powerful emotional and spiritual experiences. I recommend that after engaging with the Lectio Divina, you take a moment to write down the thoughts and feelings God revealed to you in that moment. You can reflect on those moments down the road, weeks or even months later.

Revisiting God's revelations to us during moments of contemplative prayer is a critical part of the growth process. It is also very helpful when engaging in grief work. Doing so helps us better understand ourselves in relationship to Christ and others. We can literally see moments of closeness with God that might have otherwise been forgotten and identify patterns of growth or regression in our grief. When engaging in grief work, symptoms will come and go, and we will find ourselves moving back and forth between the stages of grief. The one constant is that Jesus is present in every moment, and in every storm. I would like to share the revelations God showed me during that moment of contemplation with this same story, in the hopes that it might provide you with more room to reflect upon your own revelations.

It had been nearly a year since Mark had passed, and as I stated earlier, I was regressing in my walk with grief. My mentor had pointed out to me that I had built an unrealistic expectation for myself that for me to move forward with celebrating Valentine's Day with my wife, I had to let go of my sadness for Mark. I had painted myself into a cognitive box and I felt trapped. I also started to let my moments of contemplation slip from my routine. I was experiencing fewer bouts of paralyzing sadness, and as a result thought I was almost "done" with grieving. I had taken the yoke off and thought I could handle carrying my grief alone.

During that moment of contemplative prayer, as I sat with the disciples in the boat, fearing that the storm would consume us, I watched Jesus approach us on the water and call Peter out onto the sea. As my heart stopped watching Peter walk on water, and after witnessing Jesus holding him in his arms, comforting him and calming the storm, I came to understand my own grief better. I also grew closer in my relationship with Christ. I had experienced a moment of calmness in my walk with grief that appeared as the acceptance stage of grief. But the approaching one-year anniversary of Mark's passing shifted me back into the depression stage. It came upon me suddenly and without warning. The storm was my own movement in the stages of grief. I had briefly abandoned my yoke with Christ, and like the disciples, I was bobbing around aimlessly in the sea, distant from Christ. That's when the storm hit.

The massive waves, brutal wind, and heavy rain were my symptoms of grief. The symptoms of sadness, anxiety, and even anger towards myself were consuming me. It was tossing my sense of stability around in the sea of grief, and I was terrified that I would be unable to escape the storm. That's when the doubt set in. Just like Peter, I took my eyes off of Jesus for a moment and started to feel as though the storm would consume me. I started to dip below the waves. Jesus words, "Why do you doubt?" suddenly came into focus. My doubt wasn't in Jesus himself; rather, I doubted the need to stay close to him when the storm hit. I thought I could weather the waves on my own. When I returned to contemplative prayer, I was essentially putting the yoke back on my and Jesus's shoulders. I was acknowledging that I could not carry the grief alone and needed time with Jesus to help me process my emotions. In that moment, Jesus showed up. He always shows up.

Just like in the story, Jesus walks through the storm of my anxiety, sadness, and self-loathing to come to me. He's seen these waves and winds of grief before. He has experienced them himself. He wants to reach out to me in my moment of fear and sorrow and call me to come to him. I could hear Peter yelling out to Jesus, "Lord, if it is you, command me to come to you on the water!" During my moment of contemplation, I asked Jesus to help me with my grief. I wanted to know he was near and to save me from my symptoms.

Jesus responded to me instantly during my contemplation with a feeling of peace. He was calling me out onto the water. He was telling me he was glad to see me again, and he was eager to take the yoke. I was reaching out to Jesus, trying to stand on the waves, but the storm I was experiencing was too fierce. I told him that the waves were too big. The sorrow was too vast. The self-loathing was too cold. I was afraid to step out onto the water because I thought I would drown from my symptoms. Just like Peter, I lost sight of Jesus and focused on the storm. I became so overwhelmed with the uncertainty of my feelings and situation that I began to sink below the waves.

And it was in that moment that I was reminded of Jesus's promise: "My yoke is easy, and my burden is light." I repeated the Scripture again in that moment of contemplation. "My yoke is easy, and my burden is light." That was Jesus grabbing me and pulling me up from beneath the waves. As I repeated the verse, "My yoke is easy, and my burden is light," over and over, I could hear Jesus saying to me, "Antonio, why do you doubt? Antonio, keep your eyes fixed on me. Don't worry about the storm. I command the winds and the sea. I've seen this storm before. Keep coming to me, Antonio. It's OK. You're OK."

In that moment, the fear, anxiety, and anger I was feeling started to subside. I was back with Jesus in the boat, and he was hugging and comforting me. He was telling me it would be OK. "The storm has passed. You're back here with me."

Tears rolled down my cheeks and all I could say was, "I miss him so much, Lord. I miss my friend. I miss his laugh. I miss his hug. I didn't want him to go. He didn't have to leave the way he did."

"I know. I know," Jesus replied in a soft voice. "It's OK. You're OK. He's with me now. He's safe and he's not hurting anymore."

I sat with those feelings, tears streaming down my face, imagining Jesus holding me on the boat as the storm passed. I stayed in the moment for as long as it took for me to feel Jesus's embrace. I didn't want to leave the boat. What was once a chaotic and fearful place had been transformed into a refuge from the storm. I stayed with Jesus in that moment of contemplation until the tears stopped and the storm passed.

I learned a lot from that moment of contemplation. I learned that I could both feel sadness and experience intense joy. I felt both when Jesus was holding me on the boat. I felt a deep sadness for the loss of my friend, and I felt a peace and joy that no substance could ever provide when Jesus was holding me. I also learned that I could carry both of these feelings with me in my life. I could sit with my wife and enjoy her presence during our dinner, and I could quietly miss my friend. Missing Mark made me appreciate that my wife was still here with me, and it made that moment even more special because I didn't take her presence for granted. Finally, I learned that grief work is harder when we try to walk with our grief alone. Grief is a force that strengthens with our resistance. This resistance can come from denial, or arrogance, or even fear. When I postured myself to submit to grief rather than deny it, I could then keep my eyes fixed on Jesus. The doubt subsides. I would humbly ask you to consider what posture you have taken towards your grief. Jesus is effectively asking all of us, "Why do you doubt?" He is challenging us to consider why we think we can weather the storm without him. If you have not submitted fully to it, then the storm will return, often more powerful than when you experienced it in the past.

Reader, as you sat with Jesus in your moment of contemplation, you may have experienced feelings and revelations different from mine. That's OK and is a normal part of the contemplative process. Try not to put pressure on yourself to feel what others may feel in their conversations with Christ. I cannot promise you that God will show up a certain way. I can promise you, though, that he will always show up. In my ten years of practicing contemplative prayer, God has always revealed himself to me. Like Jesus in this story, he responds immediately to our needs and clearly communicates the path we can take that will lead us to him. We only need to submit ourselves fully in moments of contemplation to keep our eyes fixed on him.

As you continue your grief work, I would encourage you to take time to engage in the Lectio Divina. The passage we reflected on from Matthew is one powerful piece of Scripture that always speaks to me, but there are others. Through my years of practicing the Lectio Divina, I have also found the following Scriptures helpful in providing God's revelations to me. Below are a few of my favorites that I find myself returning to in moments of grief:

1. Elijah in the cave (1 Kgs 19:9–18).
2. The woman who bled for twelve years (Matt 9:30–22; Mark 5:25–34; Luke 8:43–48).
3. The crucifixion of Jesus (Matt 27:32–56; Mark 15:21–41; Luke 23:33–49; John 19:17–42).
4. Jesus raising Lazarus from the dead (John 11:38–44).
5. The agony in the garden (Matt 26:36–42; Luke 22:40–46).
6. Jesus and the miraculous catch of fish (John 21:1–13).
7. The women at the tomb (Matt 28:1–10; Mark 16:1–8; Luke 24:1–12; John 20:1–18).

There are many more pieces of Scripture you can use to guide your practice of the Lectio Divina. These are just a few of my favorites. Whatever Scripture you use, give yourself enough time to move through the four steps of the process: read, reflect, respond, and rest in your moments with God. Speak to him openly and honestly during those moments and take the time to write down your revelations. Finally, allow those moments to reappear in your daily routines. Contemplative prayer needn't be restricted to grief work. It is a tool that allows us to remain in our awareness of the constant presence of God, and to seek him in every moment of our day. Contemplative prayer leads to contemplative thoughts. Contemplative thoughts lead to contemplative observations. Contemplative observations lead to contemplative behaviors. Over the years, I have come to rely on my moments in silence with God, whether it's during my morning walk, at lunch in my office, or even while sitting in traffic. I carry God's presence with me at all moments and frequently talk to him about how I am feeling. Try to keep your eyes fixed on Jesus both during the storms in your life and when the seas are calm, and you will experience a peace unlike anything the material world can provide. Your moments of doubt will become less frequent, and faith will slowly replace the uncertainty you may be feeling. Let go of the doubt.

4

Seeking the Marrow

"Grief, I've learned, is really just love. It's all the love you want to give but cannot. All that unspent love gathers up in the corners of your eyes, the lump in your throat, and in that hollow part of your chest. Grief is just love with no place to go."

—Jamie Anderson

When my daughter was little, we watched the animated movie *Alice in Wonderland*. In one of the scenes Alice is engaged in a frantic conversation with the rabbit who is panicking because he is late for an appointment. Before sending Alice into his house to find his gloves, he yells at her, "Don't just do something! Stand there!"[1] The quote was intended to be humorous and emphasize the bewildered and frantic state of the rabbit who at this point was just hollering nonsense, but as I sat with my daughter, I realized the phrase actually made a lot of sense from a spiritual perspective. Western culture has established a norm that if we are not "doing something" we are not accomplishing anything. We just need to be doing something, even if we're not doing it well, because in our societal consciousness, it's still better than doing nothing. Much of our societal expectations are that we work through our emotions rather than pause to experience them.

When we experience difficulties in our lives, our employer encourages us to take a personal day, or bereavement leave. When you return, it's time

1. Geronimi et al., dirs., *Alice in Wonderland* (Walt Disney Productions, 1951).

to get back to business. We sense an unspoken societal rule to avoid sitting too long with our feelings and pausing routines. We fear that people will think "we're not OK" or that our grief is overwhelming us. And guess what? They are right. We are not in fact OK, and yes, our grief overwhelms us. That's what grief does. It's normal. But when we are experiencing grief, it's common for people to unintentionally pressure others to negate or move past their grief. Statements like, "He died a year ago; isn't it time you learned to move on?" or, "Let's just go out and have a good time so you can forget about those feelings," are mentioned. The individuals who share these statements don't mean us harm. Their sense of urgency for you to move past your grief is rooted in their own feelings of awkwardness because they don't know how to deal with your grief. They feel inadequate and uncertain of what to say to someone that is hurting and therefore, they encourage you to "move on" so they can move on from their own discomfort.

I once sat with a young woman who was grieving the death of both her parents. She was sixteen years old and had lost one parent to a drug overdose and the other to cancer in a nine-month period. She was crying inconsolably, and I thought her tears stemmed from feelings of sadness. I was surprised to learn that they were actually tears of anger. When I asked her what she was feeling, she said, "I'm pissed! Do you know what my pastor told me? He told me that my parents dying was part of God's plan! *How is my mom dying with a needle in her arm part of God's plan? How is my dad dying of cancer before I graduate high school part of God's plan?* I'm done with him and I'm done with God!" she yelled.

What could I possibly say in that moment to help her feel better? Imagine if I had said something like, "Well at least you have grandparents that can care for you now," or "Maybe you can go out with some of your friends to take your mind off things," or even worse, "You'll see one day the plans God has in store for you." That would be of no help to this young woman. It would be tone-deaf and hurtful to her feelings. I sat with the young woman through her tears and told her that I was so sorry for what she experienced. I told her I would probably be feeling the same way if I was in her shoes, and then, I just sat with her a little longer. When she had finished crying, I asked if I could visit her again tomorrow, just to listen to her again. I promised I would not share any resources until she felt she wanted them, and that all I wanted to do was be present with her and provide a safe space for her to say exactly what was on her heart and mind. Eventually, she came to a place where she was open to talking to someone about her feelings. We visited and interviewed multiple therapists until she found one she was comfortable with and then began her walk with grief.

Contrary to societal expectations, walking with grief feels more like running a marathon rather than a sprint. It's a long and sometimes painful process of taking small and deliberate steps towards joy. I know that sounds odd, but please stay with me. I don't make that statement flippantly, and I am not negating your pain. In fact, I did not believe this statement myself until I discovered contemplative prayer. Contemplative prayer helped me realize that walking with grief was also walking with Jesus. The two are two sides of the same coin. I slowly became aware that where there was grief, there was Jesus. Where there was joy, there was Jesus. The path of grief and joy lead to the same destination. Contemplative prayer was the bridge that connected the two for me.

Reader, I'm going to pivot briefly and share a bit of information with you related to a specific order of friars and their contemplative practices. Though you may think I am headed off course, I fully intend on bringing us back to our conversation on grief. You will see why contemplative prayer is so important in the subsequent pages. Earlier in the book, I had mentioned that St. Francis of Assisi later became recognized as the founder of the Franciscan Order of Friars in the Catholic Church. Franciscans have always fascinated me for several reasons. Franciscans are a blend of contemplatives and social activists. Their practices, inspired by St. Francis of Assisi, are focused on living a life of poverty and prayer, and include service to the poor and the marginalized. Their goal is to promote biblical justice in the simplest way possible: by living out the teachings of Christ. To adopt a Franciscan mindset is to adopt a life of contemplation, social action, and humility. Franciscans seek to find God in what is sometimes considered the insignificant and mundane and work to introduce Jesus to others through their actions. A popular mentality of the Franciscan order is to "preach the gospel at all times, and when necessary, use words."[2]

St. Francis has been noted to describe his spiritual practices as the attempt to seek the "marrow of the Gospel." In fact, he only had one rule for his friars: St. Francis wrote, "The rule and the life of the Friars Minor is to simply live the Gospel." His ultimate desire was to live out the teachings of Jesus Christ in every action of every day. He wished less to preach salvation, and rather, be salvation to those he encountered. St. Francis was later challenged by the pope who looked on his rule and writings and said, "This is no rule. This is just the

2. Rohr, *Everything Belongs*, ch. 4.

Gospel."[3] That was entirely St. Francis's point. At the marrow of St. Francis's spirituality was a recognition that God can be found in the simplistic beauty of a budding flower, rather than under the gold and marble dome of a cathedral. He chose a life of poverty, guided by the first line of the beatitudes, "Blessed are the poor in spirit" (Matt 5:1–12), rather than a life of opulence as some church leaders lived at the time; and, he favored the concept of being more Christ-like than biblically rooted. During St. Francis's life, church leaders had gained power and wealth and exemplified great knowledge of the Scriptures, but their behaviors were anything but Christlike. His goal was to guide followers back to the marrow of the gospel, and that is Christ.

An important aspect of St. Francis's theology was teaching his Friars Minor to view the world through a Christlike lens rather than the secular lens that we have become accustomed to. St. Francis recognized the inherent contradiction of Christ's teachings to societal norms of the day. It was disruptive to the political and economic systems of Jesus's time, and ultimately is what led him to be murdered for preaching. St. Francis referred to these contradictions as the "upside down order of things."[4] The concept stemmed from the realization that seeking the marrow of the gospel requires the individual to adopt a Christlike lens that leads to gospel-oriented action that is radical to mainstream thought and abandons the conventional framework of viewing the world. Teachings like:

1. "So the last will be first, and the first will be last" (Matt 20:16 NIV).
2. "Whoever would save his life will lose it, but whoever loses his life for my sake will find it" (Matt 16:25 ASV).
3. "But I say to you, Do not resist the one who is evil. But if anyone slaps you on the right cheek, turn to him the other also" (Matt 5:39 ESV).
4. "For it is the one who is least among you all who is the greatest" (Luke 9:46–48 NIV).
5. Jesus said to him, "If you would be perfect, go, sell what you possess and give to the poor, and you will have treasure in heaven; and come, follow me" (Matt 19:21 ESV).
6. "My grace is sufficient for you, for my power is made perfect in weakness. Therefore I will boast all the more gladly about my weaknesses, so that Christ's power may rest on me" (2 Cor 12:9 NIV).

3. Francis, as cited in Irish Catholic Bishops' Conference, "Archbishop Farrell."
4. Francis, as cited in Rohr, *Everything Belongs*, 62–64.

7. Jesus, the King of all kings, enters the world as a helpless infant (Luke 2:7 NIV).
8. Jesus riding into Jerusalem on a donkey rather than a warhorse (Matt 21:1–11 NIV).
9. "Put your sword back into its place." Even under threat of violence and persecution, we are called to respond to violence with nonviolence (Matt 26:52–56 NIV).
10. "Father, forgive them, for they do not know what they are doing" (Luke 23:34 NIV).

As I'm sure you have noticed from Jesus's teachings above, living a life of Christlikeness is far from easy. It requires a constant level of deep humility, combined with an awareness of Christ's presence in all things. One cannot go out into the world and hope to reveal Christ to all they encounter simply by being kind. For the Franciscans, representing the gospel is taken very seriously and requires constant moments of deep reflection. This is where contemplative prayer comes in.

For Franciscans, contemplative prayer is central to their spirituality. Contemplative prayer serves as a conduit to gaze, consider, contemplate, and imitate Christ by intentionally carving out time to sit quietly in the presence of God. This process deepens one's awareness of the presence of God and compels the heart to act on the gospel. They seek to identify the marrow in the ordinary aspects of life. So, the entire Franciscan outlook on spirituality, and their practices, align with the upside-down order of Christlikeness. They don't rush into the service of others to impress the world around them. They intentionally take time to pause and spend intimate moments with God that prepare them to keep Christ and the gospel at the marrow, or center, of all they do. Franciscans don't abide by society's dominant mindset of "Don't just stand there! Do something!" In fact, quite the opposite. They see the wisdom in the rabbit's statement to Alice. In order to be the gospel to others, we must pause and submit and reflect first. We don't want to do something for the sake of appearing to be busy, not if it does not glorify God. We want to adopt the rabbit's mindset of "Don't just do something! Stand there!"

When it comes to grief work, the same mentality applies. If we rush through our grief, we don't end up walking with it. We just end up running from it. And grief always catches up with us, because the longer we run from it, we grow weary, but grief grows stronger. The key is to resist the societal expectations for you to move past your grief or place a timeline on the grief process. Dr. Brené Brown, a brilliant scholar who focuses much of her research on the complexities of human emotions, was once asked the question, "How long does true grief last in the heart?" She responded, "As long as it takes."[5] I fully believe that to be true. A decade has passed since Mark's death, and I still grieve his loss. But that dynamic, as true as it is, poses another challenging question: "In the midst of the storms and the rise and recessions of my symptoms, how do I keep moving forward in my grief, and avoid getting stuck in it entirely?" My response to that question would be contemplative prayer.

Up to this point in the book, I have shared very personal instances when I struggled with my grief. The surges of my grief were so intense that I was left paralyzed in bed. I finally reached out to a professional to talk about my grief, which helped, but he also taught me that I needed a tool to help me take the baby steps required to keep moving forward, even in the moments when I felt stuck. Centering prayer is what helped me keep my feet moving, even if it were only inches at a time. Between reciting the Jesus Prayer, centering on Scripture, engaging in the Lectio Divina, or pausing in my day to practice the Daily Examen, I came to realize in my discussions with God that grief's marrow is love, and in 1 John 4:7–21 we learn that God is love. We can see in this Scripture exactly what the marrow of grief consists of. In 1 John 4:7–21 is says (MSG):

> My beloved friends, let us continue to love each other since love comes from God. Everyone who loves is born of God and experiences a relationship with God. The person who refuses to love doesn't know the first thing about God, because God is love—so you can't know him if you don't love. This is how God showed his love for us: God sent his only Son into the world so we might live through him. This is the kind of love we are talking about—not that we once upon a time loved God, but that he loved us and sent his Son as a sacrifice to clear away our sins and the damage they've done to our relationship with God.
>
> My dear, dear friends, if God loved us like this, we certainly ought to love each other. No one has seen God, ever. But if we love one another, God dwells deeply within us, and his love becomes complete in us—perfect love!
>
> This is how we know we're living steadily and deeply in him, and he in us: He's given us life from his life, from his very own

5. Brown, as cited in Weisholtz, "Brené Brown Opens Up."

> Spirit. Also, we've seen for ourselves and continue to state openly that the Father sent his Son as Savior of the world. Everyone who confesses that Jesus is God's Son participates continuously in an intimate relationship with God. We know it so well, we've embraced it heart and soul, this love that comes from God.
>
> God is love. When we take up permanent residence in a life of love, we live in God and God lives in us. This way, love has the run of the house, becomes at home and mature in us, so that we're free of worry on Judgment Day—our standing in the world is identical with Christ's. There is no room in love for fear. Well-formed love banishes fear. Since fear is crippling, a fearful life—fear of death, fear of judgment—is one not yet fully formed in love.
>
> We, though, are going to love—love and be loved. First we were loved, now we love. He loved us first.
>
> If anyone boasts, "I love God," and goes right on hating his brother or sister, thinking nothing of it, he is a liar. If he won't love the person he can see, how can he love the God he can't see? The command we have from Christ is blunt: Loving God includes loving people. You've got to love both.

Reader, do you see the love in this Scripture that was born from grief? God is love, and from his love, he made a promise to his creation to save us all, even though we don't deserve it. Even after we broke his heart, he renewed his promise. And regardless of all the pain and suffering that we inflicted on God when we denied him, he sacrificed his Son . . . experiencing heartbreak and sorrow again, for us. Love persevered in the midst of great pain, and not only did love remain . . . it grew. When we love God, our love grows. It spreads to others, and it obliterates hate and fear, specifically, fear of death and fear of judgment. So, contemplative prayer taught me that even at the center of my grief, God is still present.

I once heard that "grief is love persevering."[6] Yes! I believe grief is love displaced. Grief is what is left when you love someone and suddenly that person is gone. The love persists, but has nowhere to go. Like a stream that butts up against the dam the beavers built, the water rises and the pressure builds. It eventually spills over and flows where it wants until we find another path for that love. When the stream overflows, we get stuck in our grief. Contemplative prayer helped me to keep the love flowing. It helped me direct the love that was displaced towards God, and what I find in the marrow of those discussions is that he is reciprocating that love upon me.

6. Schaeffer, "Previously On," *WandaVision*, season 1, episode 8, directed by Matt Shakman, aired March 5, 2021, on Disney+.

When I submit to his presence and express my love, my anger, my sorrow, or my anxiety to him, the waters can no longer build up, and all that is left is a directed love that leads us to a joy and peace that only God can give. We'll talk about joy in the next chapter, but before we do that, I would like to share another contemplative practice that helped me continue to take steps forward in my walk with grief.

Of all the orders or priests or brothers in the Catholic Church, my favorite order by far is the Society of Jesus, but most people commonly know them as the Jesuits. The Society of Jesus was founded over a thousand years ago by reformed soldier-turned-mystic St. Ignatius of Loyola. The vision of the Jesuit order is to find God in all things. The Jesuits also have a motto, "Ad Majorem Dei Gloriam (AMDG)," which is Latin and means "For the Greater Glory of God." The Jesuits dedicate themselves and all they do to glorifying God in their thoughts, words, and actions. This means that every decision they make must bring themselves and others closer to God.

The Jesuits tend to be very deep thinkers, even deeper feelers, and justice-oriented. The order has been known to "rock the boat" on church policies throughout the centuries and was even suppressed by Pope Clement XIV in 1773, which is essentially when the church acts like a parent who puts their child in the corner for bad behavior. The Jesuits' behavior in reality was not so much that it was bad as they challenged the authority and policies of the church through their defense of indigenous populations. They gained a reputation as highly educated and justice-minded, and their political involvement often challenged the local secular authorities. The church's suppression of the Jesuits would last forty-one years, until the order was officially restored in 1814. Even after the church demanded their order to be disbanded, they continued to serve marginalized populations underground around the world, all with the same mission: to glorify God in all they do. In my personal experience, I have found the Jesuits I've met to be "in touch" with current social problems and activist movements, highly intelligent, deeply devoted to God, as well as charismatic and funny. They serve highly vulnerable and oppressed groups with a blend of wisdom, compassion, and humor that in my opinion is unmatched. The Jesuits, like the Franciscans, are also contemplatives in action with their own forms of prayer and structured time with God.

St. Ignatius of Loyola is a fascinating figure with a deep backstory who significantly impacted the spiritual practices and theology of the church. I would recommend that you take the time to learn more about St. Ignatius and his spiritual practices as there is far more to his life than I can take the time in this book to share, but for the sake of our discussion related to contemplative prayer, I will share a few critical points here.

St. Ignatius lived during the sixteenth century and was born into a wealthy noble family. He was the youngest of thirteen children, and after serving in several privileged positions of nobility in his youth was knighted and became a military officer. During a battle in Spain, one of his legs was severely injured, and as a result he was bedridden for months. During that time, his reading was limited to books written about the life of Jesus Christ and the saints. It was then that St. Ignatius felt called to a life serving Jesus. He later surrendered his sword on an altar and gave all his wealthy clothes to the poor and entered his ministry as a priest and theologian. I am paraphrasing quite a bit here, and again, I highly recommend you do your own research on St. Ignatius's life as it truly is fascinating, but once he devoted himself to living a Christ-centered life, he also wrote his spiritual exercises into a book that to this day is used as a manual of sorts for spiritual directors to guide others in contemplative prayer.

One of the spiritual practices St. Ignatius developed is called the Daily Examen, sometimes simply referred to as the Examen. I particularly enjoy this form of contemplative prayer because the Daily Examen provides a pathway to reflect throughout the day and seek God's presence and influence in all things. The process draws us into careful reflection of how God is moving in every moment of our daily lives. So, rather than identify moments in previous weeks or months where we saw God show up in big ways in our lives, we search for God in the mundane routines of work, school, family life, etc. Instead of reflecting upon where we experienced God in a big life event, like a marriage, promotion, surgery, or death, we search for God's presence in the calmness of a morning walk, lunch with a friend, waiting for test results to come back from the doctor, or the conversation with the meat cutter at your local grocery store.

That's why the Examen is such a powerful spiritual tool. It invites us to sit in the presence of God and encounter him through our daily activities. God doesn't feel so far away because our eyes stay fixed on the presence of God in the present, or the very recent past, and help us to actively make decisions for the rest of the day. God, then, is present and forever active in our lives. He's right there at the table with your friend at lunch, or with the phlebotomist who drew your blood at the doctor's office. He's present in the breeze as you walk on the beach, or even the funeral plans you are making for a loved one in the wake of their loss. During your encounter with God, you can express gratitude for the gifts of each day and commit to adjust your thoughts and behaviors to address any mistakes you may have made up to that point in the day. The Jesuits practice the Examen twice a day, usually during lunch and in the evening. I too try to remain on this frequency as much as possible.

There are several variations of the Examen, but the version below is more closely tied to the spiritual practices of the Jesuits, who were led by St. Ignatius. When I engage in the Examen, I usually try to allow myself about twenty to thirty minutes of undisturbed time with God. I know that can seem like a lot, especially when it's done in the middle of the day and in the evening, but that's entirely the point of this spiritual exercise. Remember, we want to abide by the rabbit's idea: "Don't just do something! Stand there!" I recommend finding a quiet place where you can close your eyes and take slow, deep breaths. It may help to have these instructions with you so you can revisit them during your session. Spend as long as you need on each stage of the Examen below and don't be afraid to be honest with yourself in your responses.

1. Focus on God's presence and thank him for his boundless and unwavering love for you.
2. Pray for God's grace to help you understand how God is acting in your life at the current moment. Reflect on the moments leading up to you engaging with the Examen and focus on where you saw God present in each of those moments. You may need to ponder this for a few moments. Don't feel pressured to skip past this stage.
3. Review your day and recall specific moments of your day and the feelings that accompanied them. Name those feelings and acknowledge their presence in your day.
4. Reflect on what you thought, said, or did in those moments. Were you drawing closer to God, or straying from him? This will be difficult at times, especially when we see where we've fallen short of glorifying God, but this is a critical step of the process.
5. Shift your focus toward the evening or tomorrow. Spend some time thinking of how you might align your thoughts, words, and actions more effectively with God's plan. Be specific about what the rest of your day, or the next day, will look like. These are the strategies that help us to move forward in our walk with Christ.

As you complete the Examen, you can conclude your session with praying the Our Father or reciting a Scripture verse that will help keep you on the path of glorifying God until you speak with God again. At the end of my sessions with the Examen, I often recite Ps 19:14: "May the words of my mouth and the meditation of my heart be acceptable in your sight, O Lord, my rock and my Redeemer." The important thing about the Examen is to stay consistent with this practice. Picture this spiritual exercise as building a continuous chain that leads to God. Each link is contingent upon the other to connect one end to you and the other to God. You want to continue to build links from afternoon to evening, and one day to the next. If you accidentally break the chain one day, that's OK. Reengage with God in that very moment and continue. The more you practice the Examen, the more you will discover that you will find time reflecting on God's presence and you will also search for him in the moments following your session. You continuously seek to see him within every moment of your day, and that leads you to see and experience life differently.

There will always be something urgent calling for our attention or demanding our time. The office crisis. The upset client. The email where a colleague accidentally "replied all" when they didn't intend to. My point is there will always be something urgent that can be the perfect excuse to press on with your day. But then we missed the point. We are existing outside of our awareness of God's presence, and we are simply going through the motions of our day without the intent of seeking, experiencing, or glorifying God in the process. That is what grief is waiting for us to do. Grief waits for us to try to move past it, without acknowledging its existence, and we quickly discover we will always end up facing our grief, one way or another.

The Examen is a flexible prayer as well in the sense that it allows us to respond to our thoughts and feelings on current social issues. We can reflect on current events in our conversations with God, which helps us to better determine if our responses to these events do indeed glorify God in the process. This allows us to maintain a nimble approach to our spiritual development which keeps us engaged in our own thoughts, feelings, and reactions to difficult and unsettling topics. It helps us create an awareness of our feelings that allow us to better see others in their suffering and respond in a more Christlike way.

In the context of my own grief work, the Daily Examen helped me to keep moving forward in my walk with grief. It was a means of staying connected to God via frequent discussions and reflection and allowed myself room to process my feelings and assess my symptoms across multiple points in my day. This was particularly helpful in seasons of both stability and instability with my grief. When I was stable, I could assess and acknowledge where I saw improvement in my functioning. The Examen helped me to identify brief moments of joy or peace that I had experienced just hours before my conversation with God and helped me to realize that joy was still possible, even as I walked with my grief.

In moments where my walk with grief was unstable, the Examen helped me to remain acutely attuned to God's presence in those moments of heaviness, and it allowed me to make intentional plans on how to move forward with the rest of my day. It gave me a moment to pause before rushing through the entire day failing to acknowledge that I was not OK. It reduced my feelings of isolation because I was talking to God frequently, and it helped me actively search for God in every task, especially the mundane. For this reason, the Examen, combined with centering prayer and reciting the Jesus Prayer, were effective tools in keeping my feet moving forward in my walk with grief. It made the moments of paralysis less frequent and less severe, and it helped me stay connected to the yoke of Christ. It kept the love flowing rather than being displaced, and it helped me to see that the marrow of grief was love. It was the love I felt for my friend and it's the love God has for me. When I think of practicing the Daily Examen, I often think of Fred Rogers' quote:

> Confronting our feelings and giving them appropriate expression always takes strength, not weakness. It takes strength to acknowledge our anger, and sometimes more strength yet to cub the aggressive urges anger may bring and to channel them into nonviolent outlets. It takes strength to face our sadness and to grieve and to let your grief and our anger flow in tears when they need to. It takes strength to talk about our feelings and to reach out for help and comfort when we need it.[7]

As you walk with your grief, you may find yourself comfortable talking about your feelings with friends, family, or a therapist. I would encourage you to also include God in those conversations. He's forever present in the midst of our sorrow, and it was through my conversations with God that I found myself able to continue taking small but meaningful steps towards joy.

7. Rogers, *World According to Mister Rogers*, 15.

5

"*Agapas* Me?"

"Grief can be the garden of compassion. If you keep your heart open through everything, your pain can become your greatest ally in your life's search for love and wisdom."

—Rumi

In the previous chapter, I spent a great deal of time discussing what it takes to walk with your grief, and the importance of including God in your grief work. I also made a claim that the marrow of our grief is love, and we know that God is love. Then in God, we find joy. It's difficult to believe that something so painful as the experience of grief can be tied to joy, but that is what I've come to learn from my time in contemplative prayer. Grief is not the destination. We don't have to settle for grief. But the road to joy is paved with seasons we must pass through, including sorrow, anger, anxiety, and even apathy before we find joy. In the next chapter I will discuss joy more deeply, but for this chapter I would like to focus on the path that leads us to joy's doorstep, which I believe is compassion. If grief is where we start, then compassion is the bridge we cross to arrive at joy. What awaits us on the other side of our grief is something much deeper than happiness. It's joy, and that joy only comes from God.

"Compassion" is an interesting word and as I have grown older, I have learned to lean further into the concept of compassion when understanding my relationship with God. Compassion means a lot to me and how I demonstrate compassion to myself, and to others, has truly changed my outlook on life. The *Collins English Dictionary* defines "compassion" as the "sympathetic pity and concern for the sufferings or misfortunes of others."[1] I think this is close to my understanding of compassion but just misses the mark in the spiritual sense. *Merriam-Webster* defines "compassion" as "sympathetic consciousness of others' distress together with a desire to alleviate it."[2] A little closer. These definitions are adequate in the secular sense, but over my years of engaging in contemplative prayer, I have come to understand compassion more deeply.

In the spiritual sense, compassion does involve sympathy and the consciousness of others who actively suffer, but it's a much deeper emotion than that. The root of the word "compassion" comes from the Latin root word *compati*, which means to "suffer with" or "feel pity." Throughout the Greek translation of the Bible, the word *splagchnizomai* is used. This word means "from the gut" or to have "gut-wrenching compassion" that comes from a very deep place that compels one to actively work to relieve the suffering of another person. Compassion then is reflective in nature. Our eyes and hearts remain open to the pain of others, and we allow that pain to touch us deeply in the innermost part of our soul. What bounces back is a physical response to relieve the suffering of another person. Compassion is a call and response to immediate grief that sees another's suffering, enters a space of suffering with another, and blooms into a holy response. Compassion stays with the suffering and then responds with extravagant love.

This is the distinction that matters when it comes to understanding compassion in the biblical sense. Over the years, contemplative prayer has helped me understand the nuances of sympathy, empathy, and compassion differently. Sympathy is when we feel bad for others. We see the unhoused person on the street corner and say, "I feel bad they are in their situation," or "I wish they didn't have to deal with that." Empathy is when we see the same unhoused person and feel for the person. Our heart drops and we feel a moment of sadness for the person, maybe even prompting us to pray for them as we continue through the intersection when the light turns green. Compassion is very different. Compassion is when we see the unhoused person and we feel our heart drop, and our stomach turn. We shake our heads and feel sadness, mixed with a desire to intervene. It's the nagging feeling as we sit at the light to "do something" about what we are

1. *Collins Dictionary*, "Compassion."

2. *Merriam-Webster*, "Compassion."

experiencing. It's the decision to pull over and ask if the person is hungry, and if we can buy them a meal. It's the action of pausing your day and going out of your way to enter the local gas station or fast-food restaurant and ask the unhoused person what they would like to eat and then buy them a meal. It's the motivation to become involved in social action, volunteer at a food pantry, vote for equitable housing policies, or speak out against the false and insensitive labels that people place on the unhoused like "All homeless people are crazy, drug-addicted, lazy, or worthless."

Depending on the source, scholars note that the word "compassion" is used anywhere from 38–145 times in the Bible. In the Gospels, Jesus is said to feel compassion six times. The point is, compassion is mentioned a lot in the Bible, and I believe there is a reason for this. God calls us to meet the pain we feel within ourselves and others with compassion. He demands that we meet grief with compassion, because it is the only path to experiencing God's joy. Compassion is seeing your neighbor as God sees them, sitting with them in the midst of their suffering, and then actively engaging to end the suffering. It's what God did for us when we ate from the tree of knowledge. The Bible is a love story of God loving his children, suffering when we left, and then sending a piece of himself through his Son to sacrifice himself so that we may return home. The Bible is a story of compassion between God and his creation. If we are worthy enough of God's compassion, and made in his image, then we are called to show compassion for ourselves and others. When it comes to grief work, compassion is an essential part of the process. It's a necessary component of engaging with our own grief and responding to those who are grieving.

Some of the most powerful moments in the Gospels are demonstrated by Jesus's compassion for others. Jesus touched lepers, gave sight to the blind, and healed the woman who was bent over for eighteen years out of compassion. He even disregarded Jewish law and healed on the Sabbath, all from a posture of compassion. Jesus fed the hungry masses, raised Lazarus from the dead, and ran to the margins, meeting people who were in the midst of deep human suffering, all from a place of compassion. Jesus also spent most of his time teaching others of the importance of compassion. The parables of the good Samaritan and the prodigal son were both rooted in compassion. Finally, Jesus's death on the cross was in and of itself an act of compassion. As Jesus hung from the cross, he delivered one of the thieves from a spiritual death, telling him, "Amen I say to you, today you shall be with me in paradise" (Luke 23:43 NAB). He called for his Father to "forgive them, for they know not what they do" (Luke 23:34 NAB). Finally, Jesus willingly gave up his life so that you and I may return home to our Father. Jesus is indeed the Good Shepherd who actively leaves the flock in search of the one lost and terrified lamb. He meets us where we are and brings us back to community. He seeks out those who mourn and cradles them in his arms. In all these instances, what awaits us is joy. Joy picks up where grief left us, and it binds us up in compassion for ourselves and others.

So, we learn through Scripture that when we are faced with paralyzing grief, we needn't search long to discover the Good Shepherd. But how do we begin to search for him in the midst of so much pain and heartache? How do we pause long enough to remain attuned to God's presence so that we might begin to assume a posture of compassion for ourselves and others? For me, a powerful illustration of Jesus's compassion comes from the story of the conversation between Jesus and Peter after Jesus's death and resurrection in John 21:15–19. Reader, I would like for you to take a moment to engage in the Lectio Divina again, this time focused on this powerful piece of Scripture. I would ask that you take time now to find a quiet place and draw into God's presence. As you sit quietly with him, recall the stages of the Lectio Divina, and read, reflect, respond, and rest in the Scripture below during your moment with God. Try to search for compassion in the Scripture below as you sit with God. I'm going to ask you to write down the feelings and thoughts that emerged for you as you engaged in your contemplative session and then revisit the book to learn more about what God revealed to me while engaging in the same activity years ago. In John 21:15–19 (NABRE) it says:

> After this, Jesus revealed himself again to his disciples at the Sea of Tiberias. He revealed himself in this way. Together were Simon Peter, Thomas called Didymus, Nathanael from Cana in Galilee, Zebedee's sons, and two others of his disciples. Simon Peter said to them, "I am going fishing." They said to him, "We also will come with you." So they went out and got into the boat, but that night they caught nothing. When it was already dawn, Jesus was standing on the shore; but the disciples did not realize that it was Jesus. Jesus said to them, "Children, have you caught anything to eat?" They answered him, "No." So he said to them, "Cast the net over the right side of the boat and you will find something." So they cast it, and were not able to pull it in because of the number of fish. So the disciple whom Jesus loved said to Peter, "It is the Lord." When Simon Peter heard that it was the Lord, he tucked in his garment,

> for he was lightly clad, and jumped into the sea. The other disciples came in the boat, for they were not far from shore, only about a hundred yards, dragging the net with the fish. When they climbed out on shore, they saw a charcoal fire with fish on it and bread. Jesus said to them, "Bring some of the fish you just caught." So Simon Peter went over and dragged the net ashore full of one hundred fifty-three large fish. Even though there were so many, the net was not torn. Jesus said to them, "Come, have breakfast." And none of the disciples dared to ask him, "Who are you?" because they realized it was the Lord. Jesus came over and took the bread and gave it to them, and in like manner the fish. This was now the third time Jesus was revealed to his disciples after being raised from the dead.
>
> When they had finished breakfast, Jesus said to Simon Peter, "Simon, son of John, do you love me more than these?" He said to him, "Yes, Lord, you know that I love you." He said to him, "Feed my lambs." He then said to him a second time, "Simon, son of John, do you love me?" He said to him, "Yes, Lord, you know that I love you." He said to him, "Tend my sheep." He said to him the third time, "Simon, son of John, do you love me?" Peter was distressed that he had said to him a third time, "Do you love me?" and he said to him, "Lord, you know everything; you know that I love you." [Jesus] said to him, "Feed my sheep. Amen, amen, I say to you, when you were younger, you used to dress yourself and go where you wanted; but when you grow old, you will stretch out your hands, and someone else will dress you and lead you where you do not want to go." He said this signifying by what kind of death he would glorify God. And when he had said this, he said to him, "Follow me."

Reader, sit and process your feelings for a moment. Stay in the presence of God. Record your thoughts and then rejoin our conversation.

Through my years of engaging in contemplative prayer, this specific piece of Scripture has probably impacted me the most on an emotional level. As a child, I read this Scripture verse and thought it to be a beautiful account of Jesus's interaction with the disciples post-resurrection, but as I grew older and battled with my own grief, I came to understand and feel for this Scripture more deeply. God revealed another layer of the Scripture which touched me deeply and connected to my grief profoundly. It also helped me to better understand the depth of Jesus's compassion for us. I'd like to provide a little context to the Scripture and then share the lessons I learned during my time engaged in the Lectio Divina.

When this story unfolds, Jesus has been executed by the Roman Empire and betrayed by some of his disciples, and the larger Jewish community. The disciples have seemingly returned to the life they lived before they met Jesus. While they were indeed spreading the gospel and preaching to others about Jesus's works, they were also still fishing. They returned to the routines and life they knew before meeting Jesus and were going about their day as they would most others. We'll get to that in a moment. Another important reference is to a charcoal fire. The charcoal fire is only mentioned one other time in the Gospels and that was specifically when Peter denied knowing Jesus three times prior to Jesus's crucifixion. Peter was sitting in front of a charcoal fire when he was approached by strangers in the courtyard. Peter denies knowing Jesus three times, and as the cock crowed three times, as Jesus predicted, it says that after realizing this, Peter "went out and began to weep bitterly" (Luke 22:54–62). Finally, Jesus asks Peter, "Do you love me?" three times. All of these points play into a beautiful and profoundly emotional moment between Jesus and Peter in front of the other disciples.

Now, let's return to the Lectio Divina. As I sat immersed in this scene I could not help but be touched by the events that took place between Jesus, Peter, and the other disciples. During my moment of contemplation, I was sitting with the disciples on the shore, and at this particular moment in my life, I, like the disciples, was grieving. Still reeling with emotion months after the death of my friend, I experienced moments of sadness, anger, and even numbness. I imagined sitting on the shore with the disciples who were still struggling with Jesus's death. They knew Jesus had risen from the dead, and that gave them a little peace, but they also deeply missed their friend and teacher. They missed the way things were when Jesus was alive. I imagined the disciples sitting and yearning to hear Jesus laugh again. To feel the warmth of his presence or feel the comfort of Jesus's determination and passion as he preached. They missed their friend deeply and were struggling to reengage with daily routines in the absence of the person they loved. They sat in this heavy moment of awkward silence, wondering what to do with their day and their lives. "How can they possibly return to any sense of normalcy after experiencing the horribly violent death of their friend?" I thought.

Finally, Peter broke the silence and decided to do something that might take his mind off things. He decided to go fishing. To engage in the very activity that put a roof over his head and gave him a sense of purpose before meeting Jesus. I imagined Peter being uneasy with himself and the entire situation. He's been carrying a lot of guilt since Jesus's death and I'm sure he was moving through the stages of grief slowly, perhaps even being stuck in certain stages like I had been in my grief of Mark's passing.

In the Greek translation of the Scripture, "agape" was the word used to describe the highest form of love. Agape is a selfless and boundless love. It's the love the exceeds lust, and friendship. Dr. Martin Luther King Jr. once said that agape is the "love of God operating in the human heart."[3] That is the type of love that Jesus felt for Peter. "Agape" is the highest word for love in the Greek language. The most common words for love in the Greek language (though there are others) are "eros," "philia," and "agape." Eros is the love we feel for another when we are physically attracted to them or have a "crush" on someone. Philia is friendship. It's when we like others who like us. Agape is a boundless love that cannot be shaken or deterred. Agape supersedes "like." It's the love that God has for us. So, when Scripture describes the relationship between Jesus and Peter, it always meant to me that he loved Peter purely and deeply. Peter was one of Jesus's closest friends.

I imagine that Peter knew that Jesus loved him this much. After all, they spent a tremendous amount of time together and must have shared some very deep conversations. I also felt the guilt that must have consumed Peter that day on the shore. He was struggling with the fact that he denied his best friend three times. He let his friend down and it resulted in violent and painful consequences not only for Jesus, but for Jesus's mother and the other disciples. He must have felt like it was his fault that Jesus's mother wept so heavily, that the disciples were now targets of the empire, and that Jesus was brutally murdered. The image of Jesus hanging on the cross probably haunted Peter in his sleep, and he carried the weight of that sorrow with him daily. I imagine Peter felt unworthy at times of his appointed role as the "rock of the church" and was engrossed in shame and sadness. So, when Peter decided to go fishing, I imagine that he was consumed by a level of grief that was deeper than the rest of the disciples. In a sense, he was maybe also wishing that he could return to days before he met Jesus. It would have been easier, after all, to have never met him than to live with this shame.

As I sat with the seven disciples on the boat, I could see the frustration building on their faces as they continued to cast their nets over the side of the boat, only to come up empty. "Why is this so difficult?" one of them

3. King, *I Have a Dream*, 46.

said. "We used to do this all the time! Why is it that even the simplest thing that we were good at has to be so difficult?" I felt the same. The simplest things in life had become so difficult for me after Mark's death. I didn't want to get out of bed. I lost my motivation for work and family. I could not understand how the familiar and simple aspects of life suddenly felt like a chore.

Suddenly, a man was standing on the shore. He yelled out to us in the boat, "Children, have you caught anything?"

"Who's this guy?" one of the disciples said. "Isn't it obvious by the look on our faces that we haven't caught anything?"

Another disciple yelled back, "We haven't caught a thing all night!"

Then the man on the shore yelled, "Throw your net over the right side of the boat! That'll do the trick!"

"What is this guy talking about?" one of the disciples muttered.

"Just do it," another said. "What's the difference? We haven't caught anything anyway."

I could feel the mix of frustration and apathy in the boat. You could tell the disciples were just going through the motions at this point. Physically exhausted from the work of fishing all night and now emotionally drained, they dump the nets into the water with minimum effort purely for the sake of being good sports to the man on the shore. I felt the same. I was going through the motions in my own life every day. I drove to work because I knew I had to be there. I gave empty smiles to friends and family to avoid the question, "How are you doing?" I just wanted people to leave me alone, so it was easier to just cast my own net for the sake of appearances.

Then something happened. As I watched the disciples look over the side of the boat, their facial expressions began to change. Their eyes opened wide, and they leaned over the boat, nearly falling into the sea in disbelief. "Look at all the fish!" one of them yelled. "I can't believe it! How is that possible? We've been fishing here all night and didn't catch a thing!"

"There are too many!" another yelled. "We'll never get all of these fish into the boat!"

Laughter and cheers of excitement consumed the boat. I could hear the water splashing and sound of fish smacking their tails against the side of the hull as the disciples struggled to pull their catch onto the deck. There were too many fish. The net was too heavy.

"We'll have to tow it in!" a disciple yelled. "Hurry, let's get back to shore!"

At that moment I saw Peter turn away from the catch and fix his gaze upon the man on the shore. He started to breathe heavily and grabbed his chest in disbelief. His eyes lit up with excitement and his voice cracked, almost as if he was going to cry: “It’s the Lord! It’s Jesus!”

Without giving time for the disciples to respond, Peter jumped into the sea and began swimming straight to shore. He had no regard for the temperature of the water, the choppiness of the waves, or the distance he had to travel. He waved his hands frantically, one after the next, until he crawled onto the sand, exhausted.

I imagined standing on the shore now, watching Peter struggling to stand from exhaustion. He was shivering in the cold morning air and was gasping for breath. “Jesus! I’ve missed you so much! I’ve thought about you every day. I’ve missed your laugh, Jesus. I’ve missed your smile!”

The other disciples had caught up with Peter at this point and were dragging the full net of fish behind them. Their steps were heavy and every inch of their journey on the shore required all their strength to haul in the massive catch. As they dragged the net filled with 153 large fish, I noticed they were smiling and laughing. “Jesus! Look! It’s just like old times! I’ve missed you so much! It’s so good to see you!”

Jesus smiles back at the group. I could tell he felt the same joy. He was glad to see them again. Then my gaze fell on Peter. He looked bothered. His posture suddenly changed, and his shoulders looked as though he was carrying the weight of all the fish on his back. His eyes began to fill with tears. I followed Peter’s gaze to the sand beneath him. At Jesus’s feet was a charcoal fire. Smoldering red coals, giving off warm tones of reds, oranges, and yellows, were gently smoking. The smell of fresh bread mixed with smoke filled my nostrils. I looked up at Peter to see him fixed on the fire. He was shaking his head, and he started to weep bitterly. “Oh, Peter,” I thought. “He has to be hurting.”

I imagined Peter suddenly revisiting that night in the courtyard when he denied Jesus three times. I could feel the shame and guilt that was consuming him. I too felt like Peter at times. If I had only known Mark a little better, or asked him how he was doing more often, maybe he would still be alive today. I felt like I denied my own friend the night he took his life and that shame and guilt hurt so much. I began to weep with Peter. I missed my friend, and I felt like I had a part to play in his departure.

As Peter sobbed, I looked at Jesus’s face. He smiled gently and tears ran from his left eye down his cheek.

Jesus wiped the tears from his cheek and said to the group, "Go grab some of those fishes you just caught. Let's have breakfast together! Come! Let's feast! You must be famished!"

The disciples scurried to grab enough fish for the feast. They joyfully cleaned the fish and placed them over the coals. It was an amazing meal. The disciples and Jesus sat around the coal fire, eating fish and bread until their stomachs were full, reminiscing of times past. They smiled and laughed from their stomachs. They remembered the times that Jesus challenged the Pharisees and flipped over the table in the temple. They talked about the miracles he performed and told him about the preaching they had been doing since they last saw him.

I watched as Jesus sat and laughed with his friends. He joked back and forth with the Zebedee brothers and asked them if they still got on each other's last nerves. During the entire meal, I noticed that amongst the laughter and banter, Peter remained silent. He barely ate. He sat quietly, eyes fixed on the charcoal fire, and occasionally a tear would run down his cheek. I could see the guilt had taken hold of him. He was struggling with the memory of his denial of Jesus, and now, Peter was sitting with Jesus again for another supper. The last supper he had with Jesus was a painful one, and he was revisiting that memory over and over in his head.

After a break in the laughter, Jesus quietly asked the group, "How is my mother doing?"

The group fell silent. In a somber tone, one of the disciples replied, "She misses you, Jesus. She misses you every day."

"I miss her too," Jesus replied. "I miss her every day. Tell her I love her."

"I will," one of the disciples replied.

As the group sat quietly, the heaviness of the moment started to sink in. I could feel the tension in the air as Peter quietly sobbed by the fire. Everyone knew why he was struggling, but the group was too afraid to say something that might make the moment harder for Peter.

Then, Jesus looked at Peter. I noticed there were tears in Jesus's eyes. He leaned in towards Peter and said, "Peter, *agapas* me?"

The group was silent. The tension in the air thickened and the posture of the disciples tensed. Jesus just asked Peter if he loved him purely, unconditionally, and boundlessly. Why? I was confused by the question. Of course Peter loved him. He has been crying the entire breakfast, and he's visibly upset and consumed by grief. Why would Jesus ask him this? I thought. Peter shifted his shoulders, appearing to be uncomfortable with the question.

Through his sobs, Peter responded, "I philia, Jesus."

When I heard Peter's words, my heart sank. "Oh Peter," I thought. "I know you love him more than that. It's OK, Peter. Jesus knows how much you love him. Just tell him, Peter. Tell him how much you love him. He's right here in front of you. I would give anything to see Mark in front of me again and tell him how much I love him. I wish I could have this moment with my friend. Tell him, Peter. Tell him how much you love him!"

Jesus smiled at Peter and tilted his head. Then he whispered to Peter, "Then feed my lambs."

Peter began to weep more heavily. He wrapped his arms around his torso, like he was hugging himself in this moment of deep pain and guilt.

My heart broke for Peter. "Tell him," I said again. "Tell him, Peter."

Then Jesus, still fixed on Peter, said again, "Peter, *agapas* me?"

Peter shook his head, appearing to struggle with the question again. He swayed back and forth and again. Sobbing heavily, he said to Jesus, "Yes, Jesus, you know I philia."

"Oh Peter. My heart is breaking for you," I thought. "You are stuck in regret. You are still sitting by the first charcoal fire, but your friend is with you now. It's a different fire, and he's trying to tell you it's OK. He forgives you, Peter. Just tell him, Peter. You are worthy, Peter. You are worthy. He's forgiven you. I'm sorry, Mark. I'm sorry I let you down. I miss you. I feel like Peter. I'm sitting in front of the first charcoal fire."

Jesus leans in closer to Peter and in an even softer, gentler tone he says, "Tend to my sheep."

I look up at the disciples around the fire. Tears are running from their eyes. One is holding his hand over his mouth. Another is whispering, "It's OK, Peter. You're OK." Tears ran down my cheeks as I struggled with the feelings that were weighing on my heart.

I saw Jesus getting ready to speak again. "He's going to ask him a third time," I thought. "He's going to ask Peter if he *agapas* again. I'm not sure Peter can take this much longer. He's hurting so much. He's so consumed by shame and guilt." I was worried for Peter at this moment.

Then Jesus said, "Peter, do you *philias* me?"

As Jesus asked the question, I could see Peter's facial expression change. He seemed confused by the question, and as he sobbed, he said, "Jesus, you know everything. You know my heart. You know that I philia you! You know that I have always loved you with philia. It's why I feel so awful! I'm not worthy of agape. How could I ever love you the same way you love me when I denied you three times? How could I ever deserve your agape when I let you be beaten and killed because of my moment of weakness?"

Jesus nodded his head. I could tell he was signaling to Peter that he knew this to be true. He knew that Peter meant that he loved him with philia, and he knew that Peter was tormented by his betrayal.

Then Jesus said to him in a gentle, but confident, tone, "Feed my sheep. Peter, I know how much you love me. I know that you are capable of agape and I'm going to tell you why. You're going to continue to preach about me to those who don't believe. You are going to keep sharing my love with others until you are eventually captured and tried for preaching. Your death is going to be a difficult one. You are going to suffer at the hands of evil men. But you are going to willingly face that death because of your love for me. That's agape, Peter. That's how much you love me. Follow me, Peter. That's how people will know of your love for me, and that's greater than philia. Feed my sheep. That's agape."

What God revealed to me during that moment of contemplative prayer was a moment of deep compassion. Jesus was touched by Peter's grief, and Peter's grief bubbled forth from a place of love. His regret and pain fueled his feelings of unworthiness to reciprocate the love Jesus had for him. Jesus's response meets Peter where he was grieving. Jesus sees his friend's pain. Yes, Jesus feels bad for Peter, and to an extent, I think Jesus was even hurting with his friend. But deeper than that, Jesus felt compelled to meet Peter where he was emotionally and sit with Peter in his pain. He stayed with Peter in the midst of great sorrow and responded with extravagant love.

Jesus was demonstrating compassion for his friend who was grieving heavily and was leading Peter to experience a moment of self-compassion. By asking Peter if he loved him three times, Jesus was erasing the denial that Peter showed while sitting in front of the first charcoal fire the night of the crucifixion. Jesus used the second charcoal fire to recreate the circumstances where Peter first encountered grief and eradicates them through an act of compassion. He was in essence forgiving Peter for the mistake he made and had long since regretted and was also asking Peter to forgive himself. That's compassion. Compassion is entering into the proximity of suffering and discomfort of a friend's grief and giving them the space to feel. There is a saying that "proximity breeds empathy." I think that's true. But proximity also breeds compassion. You can't show compassion for others if you are not in proximity with them. In the spiritual sense, we cannot show compassion for ourselves if we aren't willing to reflect on our feelings in relationship with Christ. Compassion is willingly joining Jesus by the fire. It's the process of meeting a grieving friend, or even a stranger, where they are emotionally and saying, "I will give you all the love I have absent of conditions or judgment. There will only be love in this place."

I think during our moments of grief, we are sometimes so eager to show compassion to others that we forget to show compassion for ourselves. When Mark passed, I was so busy checking on my friends and Mark's siblings and mother that I did not reflect on how I was impacted by my friend's loss. I tried to keep going for the sake of others, and rather than show compassion for myself, I delayed my grief work. This moment of contemplation during the Lectio Divina revealed a new side of Jesus to me. It's OK for me to not be OK. Jesus will meet me in my grief work. He knows how much I am hurting and he knows how much I love him. That's enough for Jesus. Following him is enough. Loving him is enough.

One of the critical pieces of faith-integrated grief work is to open ourselves up to the process of showing compassion for ourselves. When we numb ourselves to grief through work, substances, or other distractions, we are delaying showing compassion for ourselves. We are refusing to sit with Jesus by the charcoal fire. Consider the pain that Peter might have been feeling when he saw the fire at Jesus's feet. It took courage and humility for him to sit with his best friend. The one he denied. Peter had to willingly enter a place to sit with his feelings and allow Jesus to meet him in his grief. We must do the same. We must muster the courage to come to the fire and sit with Jesus and talk through our grief. He will respond with compassion and lead us to show compassion for ourselves.

Once we can show compassion for ourselves and let go of the distractions, our hearts become compelled to act. We can see our grief, name its source, and allow ourselves the grace to move back and forth within the stages of grief. We won't see our symptoms of grief as a weakness or regression; rather, it is a normal process of loving in the midst of great loss. Grief is love persevering. So when we grieve, we are still loving. We are just trying to determine where to place that love. Jesus is waiting for us by the fire. He is saying, "Come, sit with me and bring your grief to me. I will love you back with agape. I will show you how to let go of the pain you are feeling. I will teach you how it feels to be forgiven, so you can forgive yourself."

Jesus's question, "Peter, do you *agapas* me?" was not only meant for Peter. It was meant for us too. Jesus is sitting with us in our grief and he's asking us if we love him enough to trust him without conditions or judgment. He's asking us if we can let go of the weight that we are carrying long enough for us to hear him saying, "I love you unconditionally. I love you only as agape can." What he gives us in that moment of compassion is abundance. Like the disciples struggling to haul in their catch of 153 large fish, we will be astonished by the abundance of peace and joy that he will give us. The spiritual "catch" will be too big for us to imagine. But we have to come to him first. We have to acknowledge him, sit by the fire, and pour out our pain to him. We have to answer the question he posed of Peter, "Do you *agapas* me?" and sit with our feelings of shame or guilt long enough to let him meet us where we are. What we will find is that grief is not the end. It is the beginning of a process that will lead us closer to God. We only need to come to the fire and listen to what Jesus is asking of us: "Do you *agapas* me?"

6

My Joy, Your Joy

"We think that the point is to pass the test or overcome the problem, but the truth is that things don't really get solved. They come together and they fall apart. Then they come together again and fall apart again. It's just like that. The healing comes from letting there be room for all this to happen: room for grief, for relief, for misery, for joy."

—Pema Chodron

I AM ASHAMED TO say that if you were to ask my wife or friends if I am a happy person, most that know me deeply would probably say no. I generally don't walk through life with a consistent feeling of happiness. It's not that I'm particularly unhappy either. My default mood is not depressed or angry. I'm not a huge worrier anymore either. I don't tend to be consumed by anxiety like I did when I was younger. My mood for the most part stays calm, taking life's events as they come with small variations in my mood depending on the circumstances of my day or my environment. I believe a large part of this shift in my baseline mood comes as the result of practicing contemplative prayer for over a decade. With that said, there are some things that make me happy. Things like teaching classes to college students, sitting on the couch watching shows with my wife and daughter, mowing the lawn and doing yard work shifts my mood from calm to happy. Sometimes, when I am feeling particularly stressed or burnt out with work or life,

I like to go for a long drive in my 1964 Falcon and listen to the engine as I speed into the vastness of the desert. These things make me happy. These activities change my mood briefly, and then dissipate, eventually returning to my baseline emotional state.

On the other hand, if you were to ask me if I am a joyful person, I would say, "Yes." It may sound odd to hear, but over the years of practicing contemplative prayer and walking with grief, I have come to experience and know joy better. Joy has taken the place of happiness for me in many ways. My grief work is what led me to understand joy differently from happiness, and if pressed, I would say that I would rather be a joyful person than a happy one. There are indeed times that happiness and joy overlap, but happiness is very different from joy. They are actually distinctly different, and after reflecting on my walk with grief and conversations with God, I have come to know that joy is what awaits us on the other side of grief.

When I was a child, and even well into my adult years, I used to prioritize happiness and treated happiness as a destination rather than a mood. I thought that if I was happy, my sadness, anxiety, or grief would be washed away, but that wasn't the case. Happiness or happy moments would come and go, only for another emotion to take its place. I would return to the same emotions that were telling me that my mind was preoccupied with a deeper issue. Through contemplative prayer and faith-guided mentorship, I came to learn that happiness is a temporary emotion. It's the feeling that comes from external events that induce emotions like pleasure, satisfaction, or a sense of accomplishment. Happiness is a mix of the feelings that come with receiving a gift, going on a date with your significant other, being promoted at work, or purchasing a new car. Happiness hits us like a wave at the beach and dissipates quickly, leaving us waiting eagerly for the next wave to come.

When I was young, I used to tell myself I would be happy when I graduated from high school and moved on to college. When I was in college, I would say I would be happy when I earned my diploma and started working in my career. When I started working in my career, I would think I would be happy when I was promoted at work. When I was promoted at work, I told myself I would be happy when I got engaged and purchased my first house. When my wife and I were married, I told myself that I would be happy when we had our first child. When my child was born, I told myself I would be happy when she graduated kindergarten. And so on and so on. I found myself chasing happiness instead of joy. Those moments would come, and they were amazing, and they filled me with all the good feelings that accompany happiness, but then eventually, the feelings would wear off, and I'd be left looking to the next moment to replace those feelings.

I think that if we aren't careful, we end up choosing happiness over joy. Grief work, as painful as it is, reminds us that our lives are indeed filled with moments of happiness and are also balanced with moments of sorrow. Grief work, when integrated with faith, reminds us that neither happiness nor sadness is the destination. God wants more for us. But what does he want? If our lives are cycles of emotions, like happiness, sadness, anxiety, anticipation, and so on, then what can we really anchor ourselves in emotionally and spiritually? What can we experience that isn't as temporary or fleeting?

What I have come to learn in my time spent in contemplative prayer and grief work is that what God really wants for us is joy. Joy is something entirely different from happiness. It may sound strange, but the more I leaned into my grief and named the pain I was feeling, the more joy began to emerge. That process wasn't easy, and at times, it was difficult for me to fully understand, but what I have come to see, and experience, is that what is waiting on the other side of grief for us is joy. If we can withstand the pressure and heat of the oven of grief, our impurities of doubt, anger, and hopelessness are burned away. What's left is the clay that is now strengthened, purified, and ready to serve its purpose. Finding joy does not mean that we will never experience grief again. But when we do, we begin to carry grief differently. We mourn differently, and we even experience sadness in an altered state. In the spiritual sense, grief is a process of purification. It tests our faith and reminds us that nothing in life is truly predictable. It is a call to surrender completely to the reality that everything rests in God's hands, and trust that somehow, everything can be repurposed for God's glory. This form of spiritual trust, of faith, of peace in the midst of chaos is joy.

The root word of "joy" comes from the Latin word *guadere*, which means "to be glad" or "rejoice." The French root word of "joy" is *joie*, which means "to take pleasure in, or delight." In both cases, joy is linked to gratitude. To truly rejoice and take pleasure in something, we must be grateful for it. So, joy rests in gratitude. But when it comes to grief work, that's easier said than done. How can someone be grateful for a divorce, or a death in the family? How can someone be grateful for a move due to the loss of a job, or a breakup that someone thought would lead to marriage? I would humbly suggest that in all these cases, if we seek to place our joy in the source of our grief, our joy is misguided. I did not find joy in Mark's passing. But I found joy in God's steady and unwavering presence and response to my needs. Contemplative prayer has taught me to place my joy in something other than an event, a person, or a moment. And once I did so, I experienced my grief differently.

In the Old Testament, the concept of joy is mentioned over a hundred times with about fifteen different Hebrew words used to describe joy. In the New Testament, eight different Greek words are used to represent the concept of joy. I mentioned earlier in this book that grief was present with us since the beginning of the Bible. So was joy. What preceded grief was joy. In fact, the grand narrative of the Bible starts with joy. God joyfully created the heavens and the earth. He was joyful when he created rivers and trees and creatures that roamed the earth. His joy reached its pinnacle when he created Adam and Eve. God walked with them in the garden during the evenings, and that brought God, Adam, and Eve joy. So, I believe it is true that God does not want us to settle for sadness. He wouldn't start with joy only to end with sadness. I would also say that God also doesn't want us to be distracted by happiness either. Those are feelings that come and go. God is stable and forever present. He has always been and forever will be. He never leaves us. So why would joy? Before there was sadness, before there was grief, there was joy.

The word used most commonly in the New Testament for joy is the Greek word *xapá*. The root of this word, *xap*, means "to lean towards" or "be favorably disposed." So, when God experienced joy when he created us, we are again reminded that we were created in fear and wonderment, which in modern language means respect and awe (Ps 139:14). God created us in favor above everything else he brought into existence. Joy superseded happiness. It was the relationship between God and mankind that was special and favored. This is what we mean when we say that "God is for us." His love is rooted in joy. So, it is understandable that God suffered so much when we turned our backs on him. The fall was a spiritual death for mankind, and God was grieving. But we see in Jesus's resurrection that joy wipes away that grief. Grief wasn't the destination. God repurposed death into life. Sadness repurposed into happiness. Brokenness into restoration. Grief repurposed into joy.

In my moments of grief work, while engaged in contemplative prayer, there are several Scripture verses that have deepened my understanding of the depth and breadth of God's joy. In these Scriptures, joy is paired with hope and strength. So, when we place our joy in God, we place our entire existence on a stable foundation that sustains us in the most difficult times. In your grief work, it will be difficult at times to look for joy. The pain, when it is too much, will feel as though joy is an abstract and fleeting destination, but I assure you, joy is there. As you engage in contemplative prayer, I would like to offer you the following Scripture verses that have helped me over the years.

NEW TESTAMENT

1. "Rejoice in the Lord always; again I will say, rejoice" (Phil 4:4 ESV).
2. "Rejoice always, pray continually, give thanks in all circumstances; for this is God's will for you in Christ Jesus" (1 Thess 5:16–18 NIV).
3. "I have told you this so that my joy may be in you and that your joy may be complete" (John 15:11 GNT).
4. "But the fruit of the Spirit is love, joy, peace, patience, kindness, goodness, faithfulness, gentleness, self-control" (Gal 5:22–23 ESV).
5. "Rejoice with those who rejoice, weep with those who weep" (Rom 12:15 ESV).
6. "Though you have not seen him, you love him; and even though you do not see him now, you believe in him and are filled with an inexpressible and glorious joy" (1 Pet 1:8 NASB).

OLD TESTAMENT

1. "The joy of the Lord is your strength" (Neh 8:10 NIV).
2. "You make known to me the path of life; in your presence there is fullness of joy; at your right hand are pleasures forevermore" (Ps 16:11 ESV).
3. "This is the day that the Lord has made; let us rejoice and be glad in it" (Ps 118:24 ESV).
4. "And the ransomed of the Lord shall return and come to Zion with singing; everlasting joy shall be upon their heads; they shall obtain gladness and joy, and sorrow and sighing shall flee away" (Isa 35:10 ESV).

5. "For his anger is but for a moment, and his favor is for a lifetime. Weeping may tarry for the night, but joy comes with the morning" (Ps 30:5 ESV).

I think many people, including myself, wrestle with the idea of joy, wondering how we can be joyful when they are overwhelmed with the painful feelings that accompany grief. We find ourselves blurring the lines between joy and happiness, which happens more so particularly in the Western worldview. We believe that with our American citizenship we have a God-given right to pursue happiness. That may be what the Declaration of Independence says, but it's not what the Bible talks about. Happiness is not joy, but we tend to look for them in the same way via the commercialization of goods and possessions. They offer us instant gratification only to discover that the happiness we feel in the moment is gone as quickly as it came. We buy a car, show it off for all to see, only to trade it in for a newer one two years later. When our neighbor upgrades their house, we feel compelled to keep up with them. We live a life of commoditization filled with consumption and disposal, chasing hit after hit of the happiness endorphins until the next latest and greatest thing comes along. So yes, in the human sense, we can pursue happiness all we want. But is that really what we want to be after?

In the spiritual sense, joy is more significant than that. Look at Paul, for example. He suffered imprisonment and persecution and yet wrote and spoke of joy. It was a joy that came from his relationship with Christ. His soul was at peace, and he considered himself free, even when locked behind bars. In some ways, he was freer than many of us will ever be, because happiness does not grant freedom, but joy in Christ does. When we chase happiness, we put our joy in "things." Things fade away, break, or become outdated. I am grateful joy is not happiness because joy is not based on circumstance. Joy is an awareness of the grace of God and trusting in that grace even in the midst of grief or anxiety or chaos. No one can take joy from me, because it does not come from anyone or anything. Joy gives me peace. Joy strengthens my faith and gives me the endurance to persist even when the outcome is uncertain to me.

Reader, you might be wondering, "So what does joy look like? How do we experience joy in the midst of deep grief? If I can feel happiness, but happiness is not always joy, then how do I recognize joy when it's present?" From my time spent in contemplative prayer, I have learned that joy needs to be sought. We have to keep our spiritual eyes open for us to see it. It's actually closer than you think, but we have to work a few spiritual muscles that we are not accustomed to using in order to identify joy. I'd like to provide you with an example of a moment when I experienced joy and happiness in a single event, and how the two remained distinctively different.

It had been fifteen years since Mark's passing and his mother, Mrs. H, was turning eighty-five years old. By this time in her life, she had lost two sons, one to suicide, the other to an overdose. Her husband passed away unexpectedly from a botched surgical procedure and two of her other children lived out of state, limiting the time she could spend with them. It was a beautiful, clear day in June when my wife, daughter, and I arrived at Mrs. H's mansion to celebrate with her. The gathering was to include close friends and family, many of whom had not seen each other in years, maybe even decades.

I pulled up to the cul-de-sac at the base of the long and steep driveway. Parking was very limited due to the large number of guests that arrived. As I walked with my family up the driveway to the front door, I looked at the garden below and remembered the times I would walk with Mr. H through the fruit trees on warm summer nights and talk about school and my plans for the future. I could hear him laughing and felt him patting me on the back as he told me I was destined for great things. As we made our way up the tall red clay steps that led to the front door, I gazed over at the garage where Mr. H's woodworking shop was located. Just next to it was the parking spot Mrs. H set aside just for me whenever I would visit. "Listen, Antonio!" Mrs. H would say in a playfully stern tone. "This is your damn house too! That's your spot. You park there whenever you come over and come through the back door. You're family. You don't use the front door!"

The massive hand-carved wood front door opened with the same familiar creak I had known for decades. Mark's wife opened the door smiling and gave me, my wife, and daughter a hug. I closed my eyes and smelled the house. It smelled the same as when I was a teenager. The smell of carne asada or steaks on the grill, guacamole, and fresh salsa filled the air. Laughter floated through the halls of the mansion and it again felt full of life. Mrs. H came from the kitchen to greet us. In a crowded hallway, filled with friends and family, some I had known for decades, others I had never met, she embraced me with a strong and tight hug. "It's so good to see you!" she said. "I've missed you so much. I'm so glad you are here." I hugged her back with the same intensity but said nothing. I was trying to keep the tears from falling from my eyes. I know the hug only lasted a few moments, but to me, it felt like an eternity. I didn't want it to end. I got all choked up. My heart skipped a beat and sank at the same time. I could not help but love Mrs. H's hug and miss Mark at the same time. I had forgotten how good it felt to be in her embrace. I quickly wiped the tears forming in my eyes and told her I was glad to see her too and then quickly brought my wife and daughter into the fold.

As I glanced around the room, I saw familiar faces that I had not seen in decades. Their smiles were the same. The furniture in the house was the same. The music was the same. It felt like home. I could hear some of the guests ask each other who I was. One of them replied to the other, "That was Mark's best friend. They were brothers." They smiled at me and said, "Welcome," as we passed through the hallway and into the living room.

It had been about twelve years since I stepped foot in Mrs. H's house. I had seen her at other events and social gatherings, but this was the first time we had met again in the house I had spent much of my youth in. My family and I made our way through the packed house with Mark's wife into the back patio where I noticed two children, one in her early teens and the other just about two years younger than her, standing next to one another at a cocktail table, eating snacks. I recognized them instantly. They were Mark's two children. They had Mark's DNA all over them. Their faces, down to the eye color, shape of their nose, and size of their foreheads, looked exactly like Mark. I don't mean that they resembled Mark. I mean they looked exactly like him. It had been years since I had seen them, and when they were younger, they resembled Mark, but the years had formed them into two beautiful children who were unmistakably Mark. As I approached the table with Mark's wife, she said to them, "This is Antonio. He's been at your birthday parties when you were young, but you may not remember him. He was your dad's best friend. He can tell you all kinds of stories about your dad." They smiled at me and said hello. The daughter shook my hand and said, "Nice to meet you." The son came over to me and, without asking, gave me a strong hug. It felt like Mark's embrace. It stunned me. After hugging me for a short time he pulled away, and I noticed that his body posture was the same as Mark's. His head was down, chin tucked into his chest with his shoulders drooped, and he wiped his nose with the top of his index finger, just like Mark did. Over the next few minutes, we talked about school, sports, and their interests. I introduced them to my daughter, and they spoke about their interests as well. At one point, Mark's son laughed with the same high-pitched giggle and shoulder-shrugging movement that Mark did when we first met. I couldn't believe it. It was like Mark was right there with me.

We spent the rest of the afternoon catching up with the guests at the party and reminiscing of times past. My heart was full, and I was happy. It was hard to describe, but that happiness was accompanied by an undercurrent of sadness. Not a debilitating or paralyzing sadness; rather, a slightly somber tone that was bound up in my happiness. At one point I needed to use the restroom. As I stepped into the small familiar restroom that I had seen so many times in my youth, a wave of emotions came over me. Tears rolled down my cheeks, and I suddenly began to weep. I noticed this wasn't a sad weeping. It was a weeping that seemed to come from a different place. I felt at home, and it felt good. I saw familiar faces that were as happy to see me as I was them. That too felt good. I was glad to be back in Mrs. H's house, again and that too made me happy. After gathering myself in the restroom and returning to the party, I ran into a friend of the family who is a priest. He was a friend of Mr. and Mrs. H and had also become a close friend of my family as well. He must have seen me wiping my eyes as I left the restroom to return to the party. When I saw him, we hugged. I could tell that he saw that I had been crying. His eyes communicated that he saw me through his smile and knew what I was feeling. He knew that Mark and I were brothers, and he knew my relationship to the H family. Without a word he looked me in the eyes and quietly whispered, "That's joy," and placed his hand on my heart. He then leaned in and gave me another hug.

He was right. What I realized I was feeling in that moment was joy. These were not tears of sadness. They were the tears of joy from a beautifully powerful homecoming. They were the same tears the prodigal son shed when he was embraced by his father. The same tears that Peter shed when Jesus asked him if he *agapes* him. They were tears of compassion. I was moved by the boundless love that was in the house that had obliterated the painful moments that had wound their way through the H family—and my own heart. Love had conquered death, and the sadness and grief that came with it. In this place, which could have been where pain could have persisted, was joy, and it was different from happiness.

Happiness came from the warm hugs, and the kind words. The moments spent joking with Mark's children and chatting with friends I had not seen in decades. Those things made me happy. But what permeated the gathering that afternoon was not happiness. It was joy. Grief had been transformed into lifelong relationships where friends who had not seen each other for decades picked up right where they had left off. Mark's death had been transformed into two beautiful children who share the same laughter and smiles that I came to love so deeply as a child. Sadness was transformed into the peace of knowing that Mark, his brother, and his father were resting in God's embrace and were no longer suffering. Joy was what bloomed from the grief. It's what God had transformed our pain into. All of these painful losses had become beautiful reminders of love.

I had said before that grief is love persevering. This is what love looks like when it perseveres. It looks like the smiles of friends who once cried. It sounds like laughter when there was only wailing. It feels like a warm embrace when there was only longing. This is what joy looks and feels like, and it was waiting for me, and Mrs. H, and everyone at that party, on the other side of our grief. Happiness would end when the party was over. The joy I felt in that moment will stay with me for the rest of my life. I am reminded again of Richard Rohr's thoughts on grief: "The process of walking with grief is characterized by learning to carry a kind of 'bright sadness, sober happiness or a luminous darkness.' It is living with the simultaneous existence of deep suffering and intense joy."[1]

Reader, as you continue your grief work, please trust that on the other side of grief is joy. That is what God wants for us. To know a peace and a comfort that surpasses happiness. As you walk with your grief, don't forget to keep your eyes open to the presence of joy. It is beautiful and powerful in its own way. It outlasts happiness and intensifies the good moments that we are likely to miss if we stay stuck in grief. The best way I have found to reach joy is to lean into my relationship with God in the moments when I feel the saddest. Don't forget to tell yourself, "I sought the Lord, and he heard, and he answered," and "My yoke is easy, and my burden is light." Keep taking one step forward, every day. Crawl if you have to. And with every step, give your grief to God. Grief needn't paralyze you. It can also burn away the impurities that keep us from trusting fully in God. Give your grief to God. He will transform it into joy. Joy . . . three letters, one syllable . . . life-changing.

1. Rohr, *Falling Upward*, 75.

7

Rising from the Ashes

"Grief is never something you get over. You don't wake up one morning and say, 'I've conquered that: now I'm moving on.' It's something that walks beside you every day. And if you can learn how to manage it and honor the person that you miss, you can take something that is incredibly sad and have some form of positivity."

—Terri Erwin

If someone would have told me on the day I learned that Mark had passed that I would eventually be closer in my relationship to God than I ever have, and that I would experience a joy I had never known previously, my first reaction would have been anger. I would have told the person to stop speaking nonsense to me, and to never talk to me again. There's no way I could have understood or appreciated those words in that moment. But after ten years of practicing contemplative prayer and grief work, after experiencing multiple painful losses in my life, that is exactly where I find myself now. It took a lot of time, pain, and deeply personal conversations with God, but I can honestly say that I am closer to God than I ever have been. I go for daily walks with him in the morning, and in the moments when life seems most difficult, I step out onto the waves in the midst of the storm instead of staying in the boat of fear and grief. I have come to know joy more intensely and it sustains me through the storms of my life and makes the happy moments more vibrant and intense.

The intent of this chapter is to share with you what life looked like for me and others who walked with grief to the point of discovering joy, and what comes after finding it. Remember, joy is not always happiness. It's deeper and holier than that. When joy arrives, it shapes the way we encounter the people and events in our lives. It changes our posture towards pain, and it equips us with the yoke that can help us carry the heaviest feelings that accompany grief. In this chapter I will share what it looked like for me to rise from the ashes after the flames of grief had consumed me for nearly a decade. While I sat in the heat and pain of my own grief, the fire that was God's constant presence burned away the impurities of doubt and fear and formed me into a stronger and more devout person. What rose from the ashes was a new way of understanding grief, coping with the emotions that come with it, and a deeper understanding of God's unwavering love, manifested in joy.

When Mark returned home from his first year of college, things were not going well for him. His addiction had reached its pinnacle and had taken hold of him completely. He had failed most of his classes and I remember the majority of our conversations that summer were about his struggles with mental health, and his feelings of inadequacy and rejection by his biological parents. Summer was coming to an end and the time for him to return to school was approaching. He was not looking forward to it. One late summer evening, he told me he was going to get a tattoo. Something to know about Mark is that when he said he was going to do something, he meant it. There was no changing his mind, and he would always follow through with his promises, for better or worse.

I asked him what he was going to get, and he told me he wanted to have a full-color phoenix tattooed on his entire back, meaning from the bottom of his neck, across the entire width of his shoulders, and down to the lowest point of his back. I asked him why he wanted the phoenix. He told me, "One day, I hope to find a way out of this pain, and when I do, I'll rise from the ashes stronger than ever before." When Mrs. H heard Mark share his plan for getting a tattoo, she was not a fan of the idea. She told him she understood what the tattoo meant to him but hoped he would change his mind. She begged Mark not to get the tattoo. She pleaded with him to reconsider and even offered him any amount of money he wanted to not get the tattoo. In typical Mark fashion, he refused the offer and said, "You know me, Mom. When I say I'm going to do something, I do it."

Sure enough, about forty-eight hours before Mark was scheduled to leave for school, he booked an appointment to get his tattoo. I accompanied him to the appointment to soak up a little more time with him before he started the new school year. We arrived at the tattoo shop around 5 p.m. and Mark explained to the artist what he wanted to get. When the artist heard Mark's description of the size, detail, and colors involved with the tattoo, his eyes widened, and he looked concerned. He asked Mark how much time he had to get the tattoo. Mark responded, "Tonight."

"Brother," the artist said, "I'm down to work on this as long as it takes but I don't think you can take that kind of pain for me to do this in one night. A piece of this size is usually done over two to three days. Most people can't sit with that type of pain for that long."

Mark grinned, looked at the artist straight in the eyes, and said, "Brother, no offense, but there's no pain you can put me through that is any worse than the pain I'm already feeling. Let's get this done tonight."

I stayed with Mark for the next fourteen hours while the artist tattooed the phoenix on his back. The artist worked through the entire night with very few breaks, and the next morning, Mark stood in front of the mirror to see a giant bird composed of flames with brilliant reds, yellows, and oranges that consumed his entire back. Mark was shaking from the pain as the artist wiped away the residual blood, plasma, and ink that was seeping from the giant wound. I asked him if he was OK.

Mark responded, "I've never felt better," and thanked the artist for working through the night.

At Mark's funeral, I was surprised to find that on the cover of the program for the Mass was a picture of a phoenix. The giant bird whose plumage was consumed by brilliant flames adorned the cover next to his picture.

Reader, you may be familiar with the story of the mythical phoenix. Depending on the historical source you research, the story of the mythical bird originated from ancient Egypt or Greece. For the purpose of this story, I'm going to loosely provide the details which illustrate my topic of focus for this chapter. The phoenix was a mythical bird that was represented for centuries across multiple cultures. It was believed that the phoenix's lifespan could extend over five centuries. It was revered by kings and commoners for its healing powers, wisdom, and selflessness. According to legend, as the phoenix approached the end of its lifespan, it flew to the City of the

Sun and built a nest of twigs and various herbs on top of the Temple of the Sun. The sun ignited the nest, and the phoenix was consumed by the raging flames. From the ashes of the charred nest arose a chick that returned home to live another life cycle. The life cycle of the phoenix continued for eternity, and for many cultures, the phoenix became a symbol of rebirth, resilience, renewed life, and hope, and the balance of life and death. Why do I share this story with you? What does it have to do with grief?

The story of the phoenix is a story of grief and the joy that comes after the fire. Joy is what rises from the ashes. In Christianity, we have our own phoenix story, and that is the resurrection of Christ. If we were to place ourselves at the foot of the cross during the crucifixion, we would be overwhelmed by the grief in the moment. Imagine the wailing coming from Jesus's mother, and that of Mary Magdalen. Imagine listening to the laughing of the Roman soldiers as they jeered and taunted Jesus and gambled for his clothes. Imagine watching Jesus bleeding heavily from his wounds, pushing himself up by his bloody legs to take each and every painful and shallow breath. Imagine the final moments of agony Jesus felt on the cross as he called out to his Father and breathed his last breath. Imagine the pain that consumed Joseph of Arimathea and Nicodemus who pled with Pontius Pilate to take the body of Jesus and hastily place him in his own tomb and make funeral arrangements, all before the Sabbath. Then imagine for the next three days what it felt like to replay that scene over and over in your mind. Imagine the feelings that accompanied the disciples and women closest to him for those two long days. Imagine the sleepless nights they endured. The agonizing longing to see Jesus again. The lack of appetite. The anxiety of wondering if the Romans would come for you next. The anger in their hearts towards Pontius Pilot for ordering Jesus's execution and towards Judas for betraying him. Imagine the guilt in Peter's heart as he laid his head to rest each night knowing he denied his best friend three times in front of strangers. The grief was overwhelming. The hurting was too much.

Then, on the third day, Mary Magdalene and a group of women, grief-stricken, took slow, painful steps to the tomb to prepare Jesus's body for burial. They were expecting to have to see and handle Jesus's broken and bloody body. They were preparing themselves for the moment when they saw their beloved Jesus dead. But that was not the end of the story. God would not let his story end with grief. The women found the stone sealing the tomb pushed back, and two angels spoke to them, asking why they are "looking for the living amongst the dead" (Luke 24:5). The angels told the women that he had risen! The women rushed back to tell the eleven apostles, and their first reaction was denial. The news was too big to comprehend!

Jesus rose from the ashes of the crucifixion and he was transformed. His resurrection, like the story of the phoenix, is not a story where grief reigns. Quite the opposite. Jesus's resurrection transformed grief into joy. God's promise was fulfilled and the joy he felt in the garden when he walked with Adam and Eve was restored. In that moment, all the pain in their hearts subsided, and every tear was wiped away. The women and disciples were not experiencing happiness. Happiness could not define their experience. They were in ecstasy. Joy had entered their hearts, and it was better than what happiness could ever offer. But something else happened as well.

When Jesus rose from the dead, his message was finally understood by the disciples. Through Jesus's death and resurrection, they finally came to understand the prophecies Jesus preached. They were spiritually formed. They had to sit in the oven and be refined by the fire of grief for the impurities of doubt and ignorance to be burned away. After their fire, they were formed fully in the spiritual sense and finally understood their purpose. Yes, they experienced joy, but they also found meaning. It was in this stage of finding meaning that they found the strength and courage to continue to preach Jesus's lessons, even after the empire forbade them to do so. Finding meaning is what accompanies joy, and it too is found on the other side of grief.

In 2019, David Kessler published his book *Finding Meaning: The Sixth Stage of Grief*. David Kessler was Külber-Ross's understudy. They coauthored books together on topics related to death, dying, and grief, and his work was also deeply influenced by the personal loss of his own son. When Kübler-Ross died in 2004, he continued her work and discovered a sixth state of grief, which he called "finding meaning." I would highly recommend you incorporate this book into your grief work. After reading this book myself during a period of intense grief, the only way I can describe his message is beautiful.

Kessler states that after we move past the fifth stage of grief, acceptance, we can find purpose or meaning to the loss we experienced. When we enter the sixth stage of grief, we find meaning in the process of honoring the person we loved so dearly. We continue to heal and walk with our grief, but in a manner that finds connection with others through our grief and repurpose it to create meaningful change in the world.[1]

1. Kessler, *Finding Meaning*, ch. 4.

There are many powerful examples of people finding purpose in the wake of a significant loss and grief. One inspiring account comes from the founder of Mothers Against Drunk Driving (MADD). On May 3, 1980, thirteen-year-old Cari Lightner of California was walking on a road on her way to a church function when she was struck and killed by a driver who was under the influence. During the police investigation, authorities discovered that the driver had a record of arrests for intoxication and had been arrested for another hit-and-run charge, including drunk driving, only one week earlier. When Cari's mother, Candy Lightner, learned that the penalties for drunk driving were light at the time, she made it her mission to change the legal system to prevent future deaths like that of her child.

By educating others about her daughter's death, and through the advocacy of her organization, Candy became the first taskforce member under Governor Jerry Brown's leadership to achieve systemic change on the issue of drunk driving. California later passed legislation that imposed fines and increased prison sentences for repeat drunk driving offenders. President Ronald Reagan later asked Candy to serve on the National Commission on Drunk Driving, which further promoted systemic changes at the state and federal level. Since then, penalties associated with drunk driving have been revised across all fifty states, and to date, MADD is credited with saving over four hundred thousand lives and reducing the risk of death by drunk driving by over 50 percent since its founding.

I share this with you because if you were to ask Candy Lightner if she still grieves the death of her daughter, Cari, she would most likely say yes. She loved her daughter deeply, and I'm sure Candy wishes the incident that took her daughter's life never happened, but in the process of walking with her grief, Candy found purpose. She went on to honor the death of her loved one in spite of the paralyzing pain and agony she felt when she first learned of her daughter's death.

As I stated earlier, grief can be experienced individually and collectively. Mothers Against Drunk Driving grew into the larger organization and social movement it is today because Candy's story of the loss of her daughter resonated with countless others across the country. People of different races, ethnicities, economic classes, and regions of the country could identify with the tragic loss of a child at the hands of drunk driving. Others found purpose in seeking to change policies that had failed to protect their children and they were compelled to act with compassion to change laws and systems to prevent such deaths from happening again. Candy

Lightner's efforts brought people together who were grieving individually and created a place to collectively grieve and find purpose by honoring the lives of loved ones they had lost.

We needn't look far to see where grief has also found purpose in activism. Cesar Chavez founded the United Farm Workers because his heart was broken by the brutality and unjust treatment of field laborers. Having been a farmworker himself, Cesar grieved the plight of others in his situation and led a movement of advocacy seeking justice for migrant workers. His organization became a national movement because others who were grieving the injustices and even deaths of migrant workers also found comfort and purpose in joining the movement.

The movement of Black Lives Matter was formed following the murder of seventeen-year-old Trayvon Martin at the hand of racism and antiquated gun laws. Following Trayvon's death, millions of people across the globe who had experienced loss at the hands of systemic racism advocated to upend unjust policies that harmed individuals on the basis of race. People across the globe grieved alongside a mother who had lost her son to racially motivated murder, and they felt compelled to make a difference. It was a topic that touched the lives of people across the globe, and we saw the power of purpose, born from grief, through the peaceful demonstrations of thousands of people in the summer of 2020.

Note that none of the advocacy in the examples above could bring back the people who had died related to these events. The grief never completely goes away, but what does change is the manner in which individuals respond to their grief. Their outlook and energy become action-oriented rather than paralyzed. The grief becomes a motivating tool that is rooted in purpose. Compassion grows from grief, and love endures. As a result, that pain is repurposed into a passion that can help carry others through their own grief and lead to significant changes for others.

I think the trick to rise from the ashes of grief involves placing all our trust in God. When the hurting is too much, it can feel like God isn't present and that we're alone in our grief. We can begin to think that God has abandoned us. We forget that Jesus said, "Blessed are those who mourn" (Matt 5:4 ESV). We forget God's promise that "He will wipe every tear from their eyes, and there will be no more death or sorrow or crying or pain. All these things are gone forever" (Rev 21:4 NLT). What I learned from my conversations with God during my grief is that I did not know him nearly as intimately as I thought I did until I had cried. It was my tears that brought me closer to God. I tend to think that for many of us, we don't truly know God until we've wept. It's through our tears and pain when he is felt the most, but it took me a while to truly understand and appreciate it. My tears led me to a better understanding of God's presence, and my relationship to him. In this process, I found joy and meaning.

Finding meaning does not necessarily have to lead to a social movement or global phenomenon. We needn't start a 501(c)(3) or become a social activist to find meaning. For some people finding meaning is creating a blog or podcast to share their feelings with others who have experienced a similar loss. It can be starting a group in your church to minister to and pray for those who are mourning. It can be rearranging your plans to spend time with a friend who is in the midst of their own grief. It can be donating to a cause that honors the life of the person you lost. It can be reflecting on what matters to you most in life after losing someone or something you loved and changing your habits to realign with your new values. It can be carrying a legacy forward in honor of the person who has passed, based on something they were truly passionate about. Sometimes, finding meaning means that we appreciate the seemingly little moments in life a little more. The smiles and laughs around the kitchen table during a meal seem a little more vibrant and enjoyable. The hug you give to a spouse or friend lasts just a second or two longer. Maybe it means giving grace to your spouse and no longer fighting over the little things you did before, because you realize that having them here, even when you disagree, is better than them not being here at all. The work call that seemed so important before a loss is delayed for a moment to finish a conversation with a friend or family member. The key is to transform your pain into purpose. It's repurposing the love that has nowhere to go into something that gives your life meaning. And that process is beautiful, even when it comes from pain.

Kessler's sixth stage of finding meaning took on a few forms for me. One way I have since found meaning in Mark's passing is my advocacy and heart for serving foster youth. Mark was adopted into a loving family with tremendous resources, but he still struggled emotionally. For me, helping foster youth know they are loved and helping them access resources to manage their own mental health is important to me. Another way I have found meaning in my life since Mark's passing is to truly take time to savor the little moments in life that end up being the most significant. I do not take for granted the moments I spend on a lazy afternoon watching TV with my wife and daughter. I enjoy being there for my family. I like cooking dinner for them when they arrive home from a long day at work or school. I enjoy kissing them both and telling them I love them when they leave for school or work in the morning. I take time while sitting in traffic on my way home from work to tell God I am grateful for the fact I have a home to return to, even though my commute can sometimes be a lengthy one. I savor the moments I'm changing the oil in my car and teaching my daughter how to maintain her own vehicle. I stop for a moment on my morning walks to allow the sunrise to warm my face on a cool winter's day. I appreciate every moment I have in front of students while teaching classes because when I see students learning, it gives me hope that they will go on to make an impact in the world.

I know these things seem a little corny, and they can feel like small things that have little impact on my life, but I have come to experience life differently after rising from the ashes. I miss Mark still, but I love deeper, laugh louder, hug tighter, and feel more grateful than before he passed. I truly believe this is because I have learned to place my trust in Jesus and know that everything that is difficult in life can be repurposed by God, and his goal is always for us to find joy. Contemplative prayer has taught me that walking with grief is more like a spiritual dance that leads to a deep intimacy with God.

When we dance with someone, we find that when one person steps away, the other fills in the space. Sometimes they even pull us closer. The process of dancing with your partner is a process of retreating and advancing, but all the time moving with the rhythm of the song. For me, contemplative prayer and walking with grief feels like I am dancing with God. I would take a step back from God in my own frailty and pain and God would pull me closer and fill in the space. At times, I would step forward, looking for God only to feel like he had stepped away. I was wrong. It wasn't that he had retreated; rather, he needed me to step into that space and look for him so that he could pull me closer and keep me in rhythm with the music. I retreated, and God pulled me in. I advanced, and he embraced me, keeping my rhythm. The more he pulled me in, the more I became receptive to the dance and the music that was playing. I became accustomed to seeking him and learned to take life's events in stride. If I made a mistake, God did not end the dance; he just helped me adjust my rhythm. This dance with God took trust. It took faith. It required me to give grace to myself when I fell out of rhythm and it took an intentional effort to keep moving, even when my legs were stricken by grief. Through it all, God eventually danced me out of my own paralysis from grief and into a place of meaning. I have no doubt that he will do the same for you.

Joy is a peace rooted in the recognition that Jesus is the foundation of our faith, and he is always present and always intervening or repurposing our grief. When the storms enter our life, we can trust that God is there, hand outstretched to help keep our heads above water. He will respond with compassion, even if the world doesn't. He can repurpose the most painful loss into a purpose that supersedes our grief and comforts us, along with others we have never met. He's never failed at this, nor will he in the future. That is what dancing with God looks like. Him never failing. He only wishes to pull us closer.

Rising from the ashes requires our unwavering trust in Jesus. It takes a level of faithfulness that blooms from our seasons of pain and sorrow, and once present in our lives, it changes the way we experience grief and happiness. It stays with us even when the hurting can feel like it's too much. What comes from grief, rooted in our faith, is joy, and our joy becomes unshakable, even when the world would have us believe otherwise. Some would describe this as resilience. I think that in the spiritual sense, resilience is more of a radical love, rooted in joy. It's a love that always has somewhere to go, even when the person or thing that we love deeply is no longer with us.

Contemplative prayer has also taught me one more important lesson about grief. Once we learn to walk with Christ in our grief, we can position ourselves to help others grieve better when it is our time to leave this world. We pass on that radical resilience, that love rooted in joy to others. When we live our lives consumed by the joy only Christ can bring, we transform the lives of others through the way they experience us. Grief looks and feels different because the people who loved us will know we never thought of death as being the end. Instead, they know that we are moving on to a deeper and brighter existence that is eternal. The resilience we gain from experiencing God's joy does not take away the pain of a sudden or deep loss, but it helps us to keep that pain within a manageable perspective.

When it comes my time to leave the people I love in the physical sense, I hope they will know and trust that we will see each other again. What awaits us on the other side of this physical separation is joy, and we can trust that joy. That joy is real, palpable, and unwavering. When it becomes my daughter's and wife's time to mourn my passing, instead of thinking they will never see me again, I hope they will come to find joy in the reality that when we do see each other again, there will be no more tears, and no more pain. There will only be joy, and that joy will last an eternity. They will be reminded of God's promise in Rev 21:4 (NLT): "He will wipe every tear from their eyes, and there will be no more death or sorrow or crying or pain. All these things are gone forever."

What God taught me during my moments of contemplation is that I can help the people I love learn how to posture their responses to death by modeling how I have chosen to live my life. I am far from perfect, and I pray every day that I can continue to become a better person, but I also know that the moments that seem small and insignificant are tremendous opportunities to teach others about God's joy. My hope is that the joy people may experience when they are with me is deeper than happiness, and that it will shape their experiences in a way that helps them appreciate the small moments they will have with others, even after I am gone.

A few years after Mark passed, I had a vivid dream. I dreamt that I was sitting in front of a charcoal fire. The flames were dancing calmly in the coals and as I watched the embers rise from the flames, a chicken was slowly turning on a spit. Mark was sitting on the other side of the fire. He was smiling at me and gazing into my eyes. His face was calm and filled with peace. I wept when I saw him and told him I missed him immensely. Mark listened and smiled at me. He leaned forward and said in a calm, comforting tone, "I'm still here, Antonio." We talked of times past and laughed and drank beer together. I told him about my wife and my daughter, and how much she has grown. I told him about my struggles as a father, and how I've grown as a man. I felt a peace I had not experienced in a long time, and I told him that I still think of him daily. Mark, and the fire, slowly faded from my view, until he eventually disappeared. I awoke from my dream and realized that the tears in my dream were real, and I wiped them from my eyes. The tears, though, were not tears of sadness. They were tears of joy and gratitude. I was grateful for that moment, even though it was fleeting, and I drifted back into sleep with a smile on my face.

On occasion, I am revisited by that dream. Instead of being angry with Mark or with God for the way Mark left, I am joyful for the fact that Mark is at peace, and that God had led me through the fire. Mark had risen from the ashes, and so had I. Reader, my prayer for you is that you will one day know the peace that God has led me to. I pray that you will eventually meet joy on the other side of your grief and come to see that God repurposes our pain into ecstasy. That our tears can mean more than sadness, and that our longing can be transformed into purpose. That's love persevering. I pray that you will draw closer to Christ in your walk with grief, and that you will take his yoke upon you when the hurting is too much. Amen.

"I have told you this so that my joy may be in you and your joy may be complete."

JOHN 15:11 NABRE

Reflective Questions for Your Walk with Grief

1. If you are grieving, reflect on the sources(s) of your grief. When did the hurting start and why?
2. What stage or stages of grief do you currently find yourself in? Are you stuck in a specific stage of grief, or do you find yourself returning to one specific stage?
3. How is grief manifesting in your life? Remember the storms. Name the feelings and physical symptoms associated with your grief.
4. Have you talked to a mentor, priest/pastor, or mental health professional about your symptoms? If not, commit to searching for a professional to talk with about your grief.
5. Who around you knows that you are grieving and why?
6. Are others grieving with you? How are they coping with their symptoms?
7. How can you collectively grieve with others during this difficult time?
8. When did you last talk to Jesus about your grief? Did you listen long enough for a response?
9. What contemplative prayer practice from this book can you begin to use daily in your walk with grief? What days and times will you commit to engaging in contemplative prayer?
10. What have you learned about yourself and your walk with grief during your time in contemplative prayer? You can use the note pages after this section of the book to record your thoughts.

11. How is contemplative prayer changing your posture towards grief? In other words, where have you experienced strength and resilience in your walk with Christ?
12. When did you last show compassion for yourself when walking with your grief? What does self-compassion look like for you?
13. If you are helping someone who is walking with grief, in what ways are you demonstrating compassion to them?
14. Where have you experienced joy in your walk with grief? How do you know you are experiencing joy instead of happiness?
15. Have you made time to reflect on the joy in your life, even in the midst of great suffering? How can you search for joy *and* continue to walk with grief?
16. Have you found meaning after experiencing a painful loss? In what ways do you find meaning in honoring the person or thing you lost?
17. What sense of purpose or meaning may God be revealing to you during contemplative prayer during this season of grief?

About the Author

Dr. Antonio Méjico Jr. was born in Los Angeles, California, and his parents later settled in Colton, California. Dr. Méjico earned his Bachelor of Arts in Sociology, Master of Arts in Education Counseling K–12, and Doctor of Education in Leadership for Educational Justice from the University of Redlands. Dr. Méjico has served in the fields of child welfare, education, and mental health for over twenty-three years. During that time, he has provided direct case management to children with complex needs who have experienced acute maltreatment, including initiated gang youth in Orange County and the Inland Empire.

Later in his career, Dr. Méjico served in executive leadership roles in nonprofit child welfare settings, successfully leading teams to build and expand upon existing programs to support foster and other adjudicated youth. He also participated in state work groups to advance equitable child welfare policies impacting adjudicated youth. He later transitioned into Christian higher education with the desire to contribute to the professional development and spiritual formation of highly competent social workers and helping professionals.

Dr. Méjico serves as the associate dean for the Division of Social Work, and an associate professor of social work at California Baptist University. Antonio's expertise lies in teaching courses rooted in diversity, cultural humility and responsiveness, organizational leadership, and faith-integrated teaching practices. He provides consultation and training on cultural humility and responsiveness to leaders and practitioners within child welfare, education, and juvenile justice settings, as well as church leaders and their congregations, and serves on multiple boards with secular and faith-based organizations throughout the Inland Empire.

Bibliography

American Psychological Association. “Grief.” https://www.apa.org/topics/grief.

Bouma-Prediger, S., et al. *Beyond Homelessness: Christian Faith in a Culture of Displacement*. 15th ann. ed. Grand Rapids: Eerdmans, 2023.

Bourgeault, Cynthia. *The Heart of Centering Prayer: Nondual Christianity in Theory and Practice*. Boulder, CO: Shambhala, 2016.

Boyle, Gregory. *Barking to the Choir: The Power of Radical Kinship*. New York: Simon & Schuster, 2017.

———. *Tattoos on the Heart: The Power of Boundless Compassion*. New York: Free Press, 2010.

Brown, Brenè. *Atlas of the Heart: Mapping Meaningful Connection and the Language of Human Experience*. New York: Random House, 2021.

Bucko, Adam. *Let Your Heartbreak Be Your Guide: Lessons in Engaged Contemplation*. Maryknoll, NY: Orbis, 2022.

Burton-Christie, Douglas. *The Word in the Desert: Scripture and the Quest for Holiness in Early Christian Monasticism*. Oxford: Oxford University Press, 1993.

Cohen, Jill S. “Grief Quotes to Help Grievers Understand and Heal Grief.” Jill Cohen, NYC Grief Counselor. https://www.jillgriefcounselor.com/blog/some-quotes-for-reflection-on-grief.

Collins Dictionary. “Compassion.” https://www.collinsdictionary.com/us/dictionary/english/compassion.

———. “Grief.” https://www.collinsdictionary.com/us/dictionary/english/grief.

Erford, Bradley T., et al. *Thirty-Five Techniques Every Counselor Should Know*. London: Pearson, 2009.

Gallagher, Timothy. *Meditation and Contemplation: An Ignatian Guide to Praying with Scripture*. New York: Crossroad, 2008.

Geronimi, Clyde, et al., dirs. *Alice in Wonderland*. Walt Disney Productions, 1951.

Ignatius. *The Spiritual Exercises of Saint Ignatius: A Translation and Commentary*. Translated by G. E. Ganss. Chicago: Loyola University Press, 1991.

Irish Catholic Bishops’ Conference. “Archbishop Farrell: ‘God’s Compassion Moved in Francis’ Life and Brought Healing and Comfort to Those He Encountered.’” November 26, 2023. https://www.catholicbishops.ie/2023/11/26/archbishop-farrell-gods-compassion-moved-in-francis-life-and-brought-healing-and-comfort-to-those-he-encountered/.

Lawrence. *The Practice of the Presence of God*. Translated by J. J. Delaney. Peabody, MA: Hendrickson, 2003.

MADD. "MADD History." https://madd.org/our-history/.

McGuckin, J. A., ed. and trans. *The Book of Mystical Chapters: Meditations on the Soul's Ascent from the Desert Fathers and Other Early Christian Contemplatives.* Boulder, CO: Shambhala, 2003.

Merriam-Webster. "Compassion." https://www.merriam-webster.com/dictionary/compassion.

———. "Grief." https://www.merriam-webster.com/dictionary/grief.

Kent, Louis M. *Legends of the Phoenix: The Rebirth Mythos.* N.p.: pub. by author, 2025.

Kessler, David. *Finding Meaning: The Sixth Stage of Grief.* New York: Scribner, 2019.

King, Martin Luther Jr. *I Have a Dream: Writings and Speeches That Changed the World.* Edited by J. M. Washington. New York: HarperCollins, 1991.

Kübler-Ross, Elisabeth. *On Death and Dying.* New York: Macmillan, 1969.

Méjico, Antonio Jr., and Terence Lester. *The Way of Love: Biblical Reflections on Oneness, Hope, and Extravagant Love in Divided Times.* N.p.: Kindle Direct, 2025.

Ramon. *Franciscan Spirituality: Following St. Francis Today.* London: SPCK, 1994.

Rogers, Fred. *The World According to Mister Rogers: Important Things to Remember.* New York: Hyperion, 2005.

Rohr, Richard. *Falling Upward: A Spirituality for the Two Halves of Life.* San Fransisco: Jossey-Bass, 2011.

Schaeffer, Jac. "Previously On." *WandaVision,* season 1, episode 8. Directed by Matt Shakman. Aired March 5, 2021, on Disney+.

Thibodeaux, Mark E. *Reimagining the Ignatian Examen: Fresh Ways to Pray from Your Day.* Chicago: Loyola, 2014.

Weisholtz, Drew. "Brené Brown Opens Up About How Long Grief Lasts: 'It Takes as Long as It Takes.'" *Today,* March 31, 2022. https://www.today.com/health/mind-body/brene-brown-talks-long-grief-lasts-rcna22395.

Youssef, Elyane S. "Elizabeth Gilbert Explains Grief in the Best Possible Way." Elephant Journal, July 12, 2018. https://www.elephantjournal.com/2018/07/elizabeth-gilbert-explains-grief-in-the-best-possible-way/#:~:text=Not%20only%20are%20we%20not,emotions%20become%20our%20best%20allies.

www.ingramcontent.com/pod-product-compliance
Lightning Source LLC
LaVergne TN
LVHW020637100826
845148LV00012B/2222